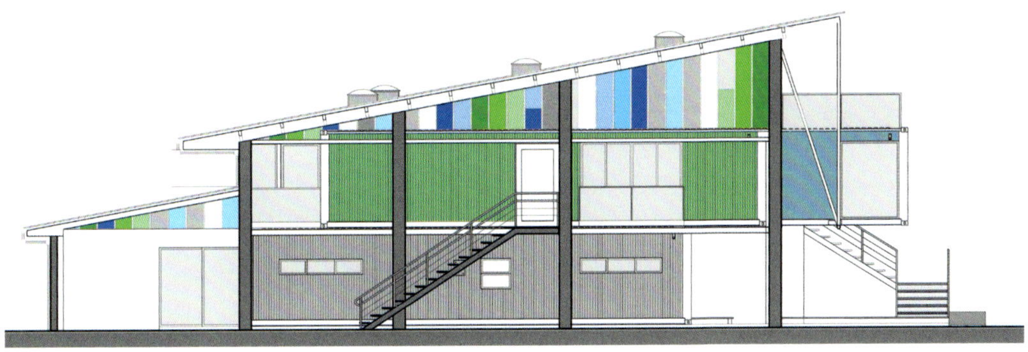

Editorial project:
© 2023 **booq** publishing, S.L.
c/ Domènech, 7-9, 2º 1ª
08012 Barcelona, Spain
T: +34 93 268 80 88
www.loftpublications.com

ISBN 978-84-9936-662-3 [EN]

ISBN 978-84-9936-652-4 [DE]

© Éditions du Layeur
Dépôt Légal : janvier 2023
Espagne, en janvier 2023

ISBN 978-2-38378-030-4

monsa publications
© 2023 Instituto Monsa de ediciones, S.L.
c/ Gravina, 43
08930 Sant Adrià de Besós, Barcelona, Spain
T: +34 93 381 00 93
www.monsa.com
monsa@monsa.com

ISBN: 978-84-17557-62-1

Editorial coordinator:
Claudia Martínez Alonso

Art director:
Mireia Casanovas Soley

Editor:
David Andreu Bach

Layout:
Cristina Simó Perales

Translation:
© **booq** publishing, S.L.

Printing in Spain

F56

POTTERS LANE

Hektor
Container

Architecture with Containers is a form of sustainable architecture creating a very peculiar aesthetic from recycled material. It is a construction procedure based on the assembly of modular elements, in this case, containers used in maritime and rail transport of goods that have become popular with architects over the past decade. Containers are robust, durable, economical, easily transportable, adaptable and sustainable. Their versatility makes them adaptable to the most diverse scales and needs: single-family and collective housing, shopping centers, offices, schools, hotels, restaurants, shelters, laboratories and works of ephemeral architecture. Eighteen architects and their most relevant projects that illustrate the magnitude of shipping-container architecture and its modular, pre fab, affordable, movable and sustainable attributes.

Architektur mit Containern ist eine Form der nachhaltigen Architektur, die aus recyceltem Material eine ganz besondere Ästhetik schafft. Es handelt sich um ein Bauverfahren, das auf dem Zusammenbau modularer Elemente beruht, in diesem Fall Container, die im See- und Schienentransport von Gütern verwendet werden und im letzten Jahrzehnt bei Architekten sehr beliebt geworden sind. Container sind robust, langlebig, wirtschaftlich, leicht zu transportieren, anpassungsfähig und nachhaltig. Durch ihre Vielseitigkeit lassen sie sich an die unterschiedlichsten Maßstäbe und Bedürfnisse anpassen: Einfamilien- und Gemeinschaftshäuser, Einkaufszentren, Büros, Schulen, Hotels, Restaurants, Schutzräume, Labors und Werke der flüchtigen Architektur. Achtzehn Architekten und ihre wichtigsten Projekte, die das Ausmaß der Schiffscontainer-Architektur und ihre modularen, vorgefertigten, erschwinglichen, beweglichen und nachhaltigen Eigenschaften veranschaulichen.

L'architecture avec conteneurs est une forme d'architecture durable créant une esthétique très particulière à partir de matériaux recyclés. Il s'agit d'un procédé de construction basé sur l'assemblage d'éléments modulaires, en l'occurrence des conteneurs utilisés dans le transport maritime et ferroviaire de marchandises qui sont devenus populaires auprès des architectes au cours de la dernière décennie. Les conteneurs sont robustes, durables, économiques, facilement transportables, adaptables et durables. Leur polyvalence les rend adaptables aux échelles et aux besoins les plus divers : logements individuels et collectifs, centres commerciaux, bureaux, écoles, hôtels, restaurants, abris, laboratoires et œuvres d'architecture éphémère. Dix-huit architectes et leurs projets les plus pertinents qui illustrent l'ampleur de l'architecture de conteneurs maritimes et ses attributs modulaires, préfabriqués, abordables, mobiles et durables.

La arquitectura con contenedores es una forma de arquitectura sostenible que crea una estética muy peculiar a partir de material reciclado. Se trata de un procedimiento de construcción basado en el ensamblaje de elementos modulares, en este caso, contenedores utilizados en el transporte marítimo y ferroviario de mercancías que se han popularizado entre los arquitectos en la última década. Los contenedores son robustos, duraderos, económicos, fácilmente transportables, adaptables y sostenibles. Su versatilidad los hace adaptables a las más diversas escalas y necesidades: viviendas unifamiliares y colectivas, centros comerciales, oficinas, escuelas, hoteles, restaurantes, refugios, laboratorios y obras de arquitectura efímera. Dieciocho arquitectos y sus proyectos más relevantes que ilustran la magnitud de la arquitectura de contenedores marítimos y sus características modulares, prefabricados, asequibles, móviles y sostenibles.

ARCHIMONTAGE DESIGN FIELDS SOPHISTICATED

**Cherngchai Riawruangsangkul,
Thanakit Wiriyasathit**

Archimontage Design Fields Sophisticated is a micro office located in Nonthaburi, Thailand. Founded in 2007 by Cherngchai Riawruangsangkul, it specialises in architectural design, interior design and related fields for buildings of various sizes in urban area. The goals are to find alternatives for design that are not limited to conventional method and solution, to seek new options that open opportunity for architect (designer) to create new experience for both building owner (user) and society or people around it (observer) and to conduct cross-disciplinary experimentation to find new, unique and special ways for design.

www.archimontage.net

Archimontage Design Fields Sophisticated ist ein Mikro-Büro in Nonthaburi, Thailand. Das 2007 von Cherngchai Riawruangsangkul gegründete Unternehmen hat sich auf die architektonische Gestaltung, die Innenarchitektur und verwandte Bereiche für Gebäude unterschiedlicher Größe in städtischen Gebieten spezialisiert. Ziel ist es, Gestaltungsalternativen zu finden, die sich nicht auf konventionelle Methoden und Lösungen beschränken, neue Optionen zu suchen, die dem Architekten (Designer) die Möglichkeit geben, eine neue Erfahrung sowohl für den Bauherrn (Nutzer) als auch für die umgebende Gesellschaft oder die Menschen (Betrachter) zu schaffen, und interdisziplinär zu experimentieren, um neue, einzigartige und besondere Formen der Gestaltung zu finden.

Archimontage Design Fields Sophisticated est un micro-bureau situé à Nonthaburi, en Thaïlande. Fondée en 2007 par Cherngchai Riawruangsangkul, elle est spécialisée dans la conception architecturale, la décoration intérieure et les domaines connexes pour des bâtiments de différentes tailles en zone urbaine. Ses objectifs sont de trouver des alternatives de conception qui ne se limitent pas aux méthodes et solutions conventionnelles, de rechercher de nouvelles options qui donnent à l'architecte (concepteur) l'occasion de créer une nouvelle expérience tant pour le propriétaire du bâtiment (utilisateur) que pour la société ou les personnes environnantes (observateur), et de mener une expérimentation interdisciplinaire pour trouver des formes de conception nouvelles, uniques et spéciales.

Archimontage Design Fields Sophisticated es un microdespacho situado en Nonthaburi, Tailandia. Fundada en 2007 por Cherngchai Riawruangsangkul, está especializada en diseño arquitectónico, interiorismo y campos afines para edificios de diversos tamaños en zonas urbanas. Sus objetivos son encontrar alternativas de diseño que no se limiten a los métodos y soluciones convencionales, buscar nuevas opciones que brinden al arquitecto (diseñador) la oportunidad de crear una nueva experiencia tanto para el propietario del edificio (usuario) como para la sociedad o las personas de su entorno (observador) y llevar a cabo una experimentación interdisciplinar para encontrar formas nuevas, únicas y especiales de diseño.

MUANGTHONGTHANI CARCARE

Nonthaburi, Thailand | Photos: © Chaovarith Poonphol Photography

The building is located on a 300 m^2 plot of land. This long and narrow plot requires an in-depth organization of the building. The façade of the building faces south while the other side faces east The neighboring building is a car care center which belongs to the same owner. Since the space of the car care center is too limited, mainly because of the closed coating area where protection from dust is much needed, a new space is necessary for project expansion.
This project is in Muang Thong Thani, a large community in Nonthaburi, a suburb of Bangkok. The building consists of 4 small containers (2.34x2.40x6.00) and 4 large containers (2.34x2.40x12.00). The ground floor provides space for a coating area, parking and storage. The second floor is planned for a restaurant with a separate multi-purpose area for a future bar. There is a stairway outside the building for customers who may not wish to walk pass the car care service inside the building. The third floor is an office. The total utility space is 330 m^2. The building exterior is painted in matte black but the interior is white as the two colours create different perceptions. The inner most part is a residential area for staff.

Das Gebäude befindet sich auf einem Grundstück von 300 m^2. Das lange und schmale Grundstück erfordert eine tiefgreifende Organisation des Gebäudes. Die Fassade des Gebäudes ist nach Süden ausgerichtet, während die andere Seite nach Osten zeigt. Das Nachbargebäude ist ein Autopflegezentrum, das demselben Eigentümer gehört. Da der Raum des Autopflegezentrums zu begrenzt ist, vor allem wegen des geschlossenen Verkleidungsbereichs, in dem Staubschutz sehr wichtig ist, war ein neuer Raum für die Erweiterung des Projekts in Muang Thong Thani, einer großen Gemeinde in Nonthaburi, einem Vorort von Bangkok, unerlässlich. Das Gebäude be steht aus 4 kleinen (2,34x2,40x6,00) und 4 großen (2,34x2,40x12,00) Containern. Das Erdgeschoss bietet Platz für einen Abstellraum, Parkplätze und Lagerräume. Das erste Stockwerk ist für ein Restaurant mit einem separaten Mehrzweckbereich für eine zukünftige Bar vorgesehen. Es gibt eine Treppe außerhalb des Gebäudes für Kunden, die nicht an der Autopflege im Gebäude vorbeigehen wollen. Im dritten Stock befindet sich ein Büro. Die Gesamtnutzfläche beträgt 330 m^2. Das Äußere des Gebäudes ist mattschwarz gestrichen, während das Innere weiß ist, so dass die beiden Farben unterschiedliche Wahrnehmungen hervorrufen. Der innerste Teil ist ein Wohnbereich für das Personal.

Le bâtiment est situé sur un terrain de 300 m^2. Cette parcelle longue et étroite nécessite une organisation en profondeur du bâtiment. La façade du bâtiment est orientée vers le sud, tandis que l'autre côté est orienté vers l'est. Le bâtiment voisin est un centre de soins automobiles appartenant au même propriétaire. L'espace du centre d'entretien automobile étant trop limité, principalement en raison de la zone de revêtement fermée où la protection contre la poussière est très nécessaire, un nouvel espace était indispensable pour l'extension du projet qui est situé à Muang Thong Thani, une grande communauté à Nonthaburi, une banlieue de Bangkok. Le bâtiment est composé de 4 petits (2,34x2,40x6,00) et 4 grands (2,34x2,40x12,00) conteneurs. Le rez-de-chaussée offre de l'espace pour une zone d'accueil, un parking et un stockage. Le premier étage est prévu pour un restaurant avec un espace séparé polyvalent pour un futur bar. Il y a un escalier à l'extérieur du bâtiment pour les clients qui ne souhaitent pas passer devant le service d'entretien des voitures à l'intérieur du bâtiment. Le troisième étage est occupé par un bureau. L'espace total utilisable est de 330 m^2. L'extérieur du bâtiment est peint en noir mat, mais l'intérieur est blanc, les deux couleurs créant des perceptions différentes. La partie la plus intérieure est une zone résidentielle pour le personnel.

El edificio está situado en una parcela de 300 m^2. Esta parcela larga y estrecha requiere una organización en profundidad del edificio. La fachada del edificio está orientada al sur, mientras que el otro lado da al este. El edificio vecino es un centro de atención al automóvil que pertenece al mismo propietario. Dado que el espacio del centro de cuidado de coches es demasiado limitado, principalmente por la zona de revestimiento cerrada donde es muy necesaria la protección contra el polvo, se hacía indispensable un nuevo espacio para la ampliación del proyecto que se encuentra en Muang Thong Thani, una gran comunidad de Nonthaburi, un suburbio de Bangkok. El edificio consta de 4 contenedores pequeños (2,34x2,40x6,00) y 4 grandes (2,34x2,40x12,00). La planta baja ofrece espacio para una zona de revestimiento, aparcamiento y almacenamiento. La segunda planta está prevista para un restaurante con una zona polivalente separada para un futuro bar. Hay una escalera fuera del edificio para los clientes que no deseen pasar por delante del servicio de cuidado de coches dentro del edificio. La tercera planta está ocupada por una oficina. El espacio útil total es de 330 m^2. El exterior del edificio está pintado en negro mate, pero el interior es blanco, los dos colores creando percepciones diferentes. La parte más interior es una zona residencial para el personal.

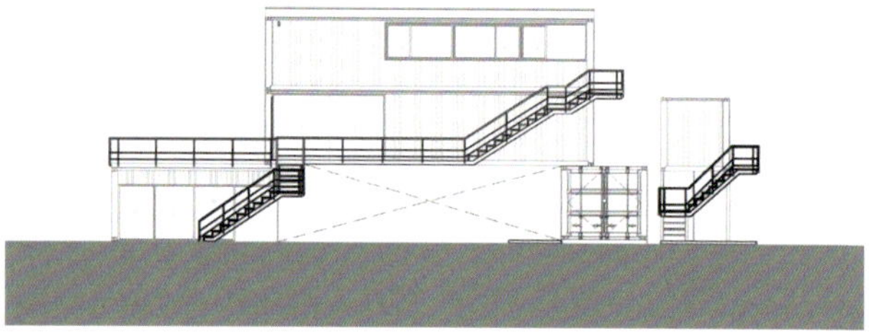

East elevation

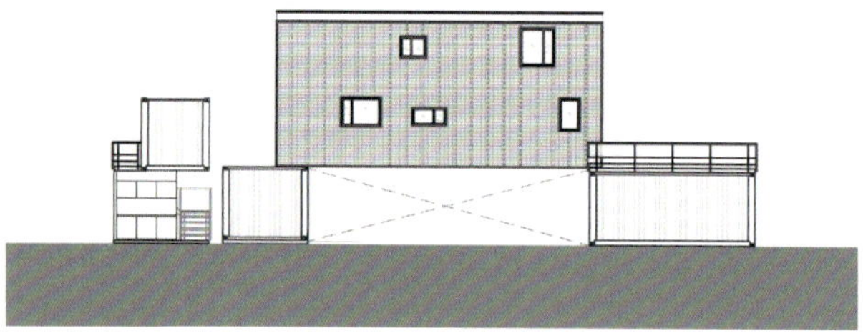

West elevation

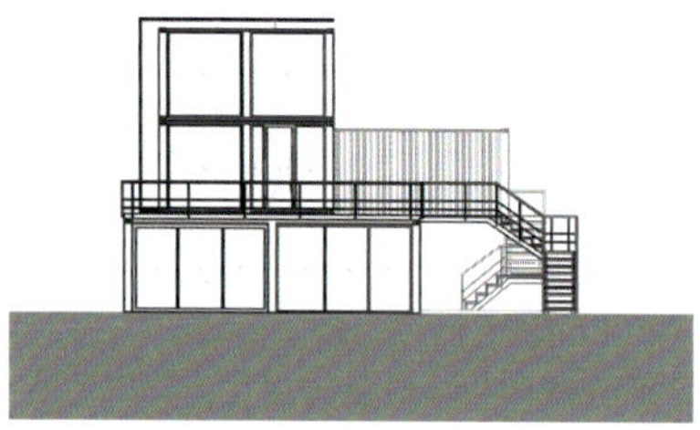

South elevation

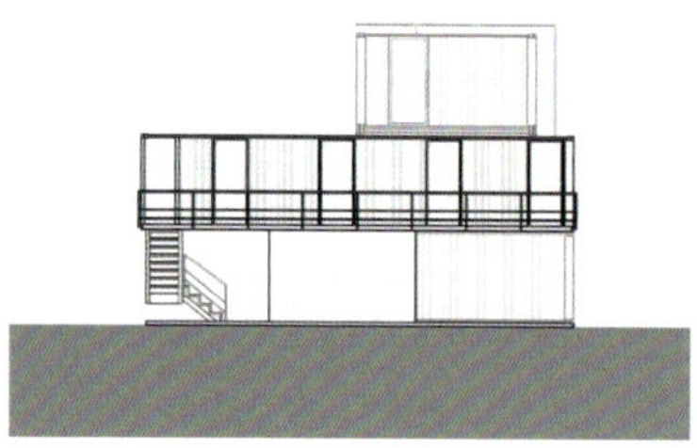

North elevation

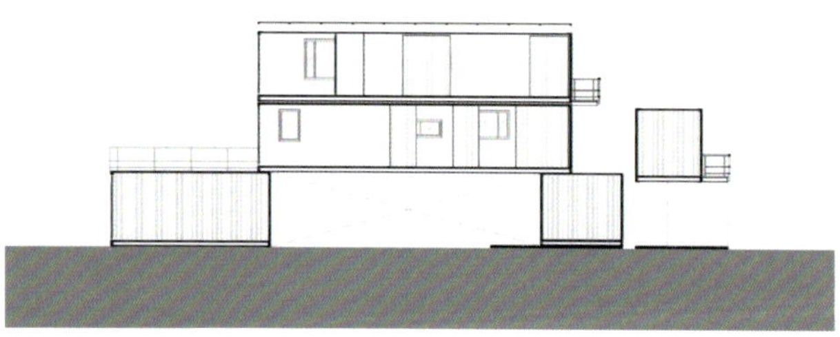

A-A section

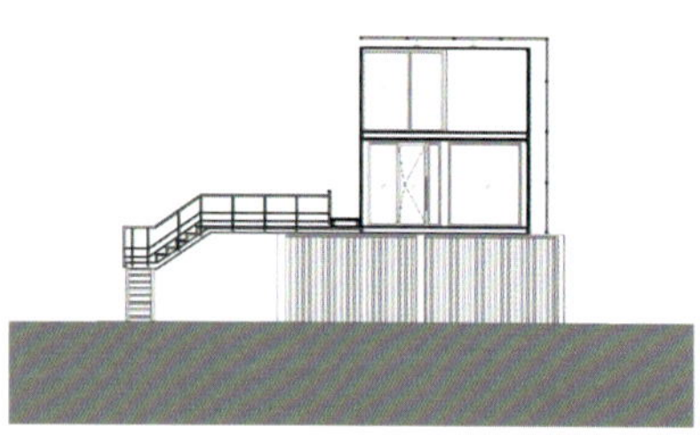

B-B section

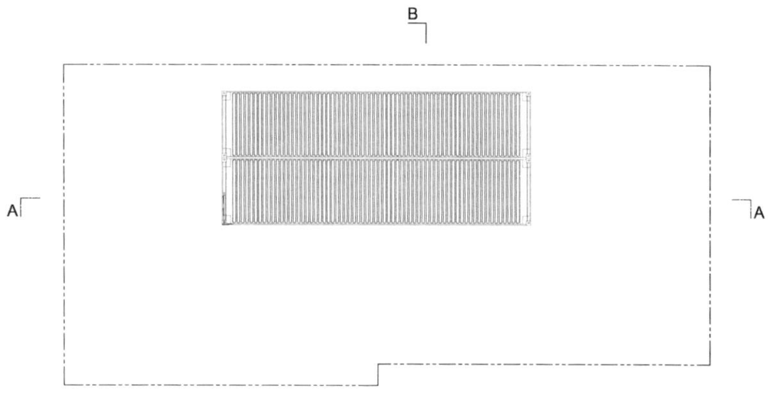

Roof plan

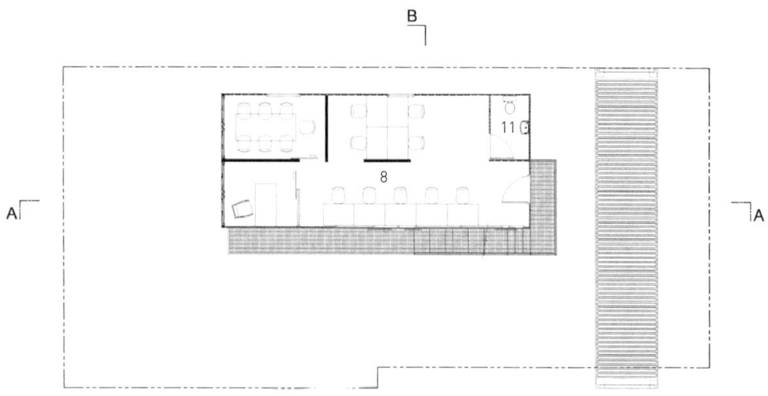

Third floor plan

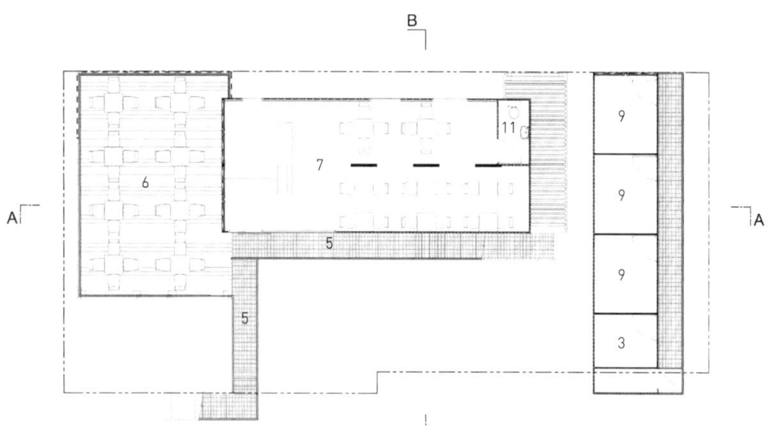

Second floor plan

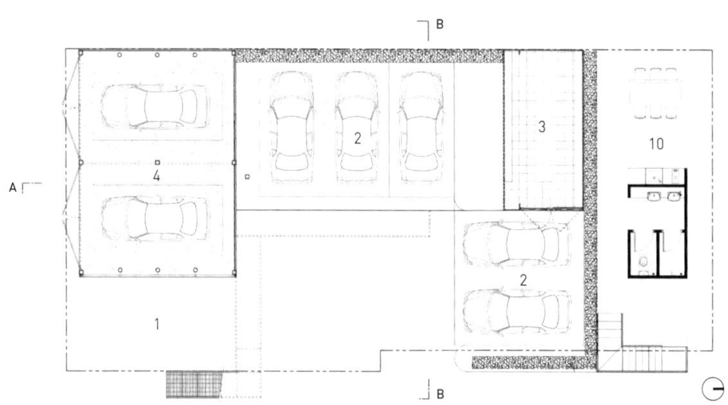

First floor plan

1. Entrance
2. Parking
3. Storage
4. Carcare
5. Walk way
6. Terrace
7. Bar
8. Office
9. Bedroom
10. Dining
11. WC

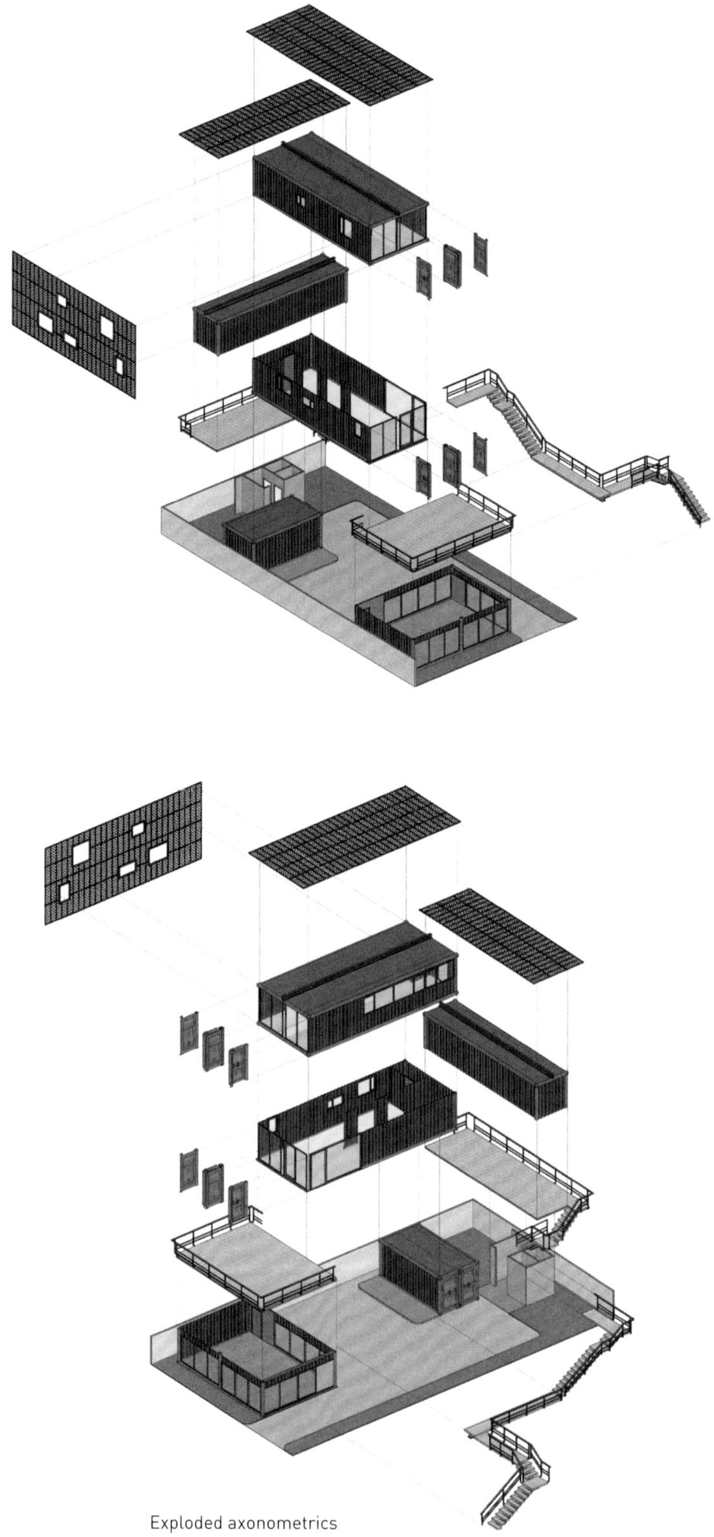
Exploded axonometrics

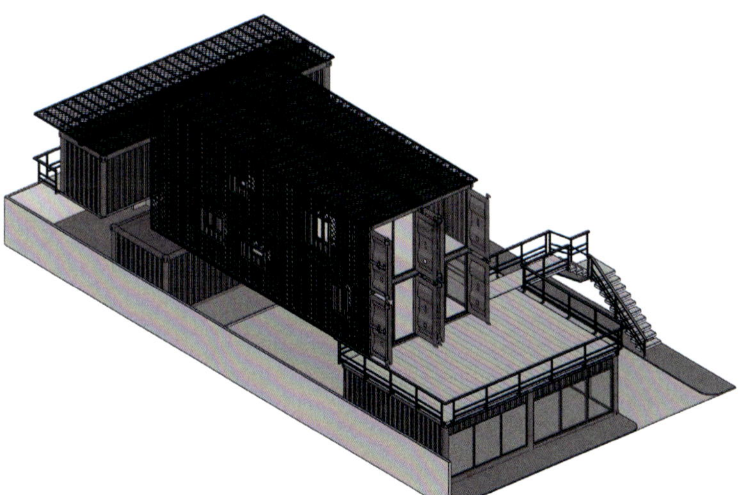

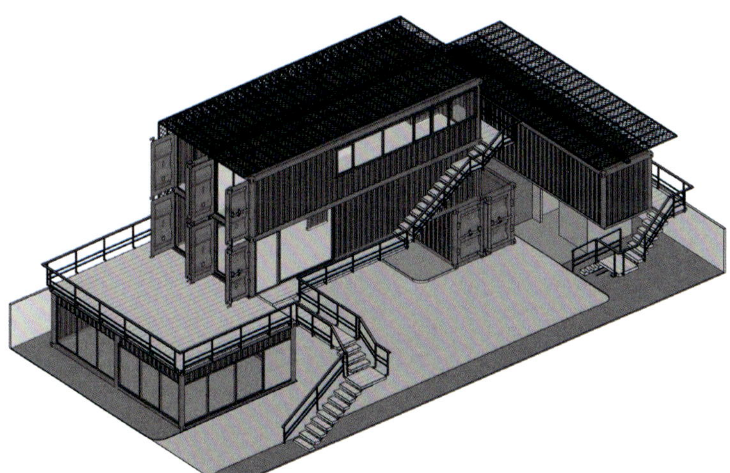

Axonometries

BARAN STUDIO

Matt Baran

MACARTHUR ANNEX

Oakland, California, United States | Photos: © Bénédicte Lassalle

The project consists of 33 used shipping containers that are configured to respond to programmatic and contextual parameters. The resultant framework allows for individual expression and simultaneously, communal interaction.

The modules carry the potential to be reconfigured, or removed and relocated, allowing for future modification and adaptation.

The project is connected to various contexts that include existing structures, the network of containers that run through Oakland, and the local community of creative entrepreneurs. The underlying containers created a canvas, and a community has populated the project with their own modifications, according to their own needs. The results are dramatically different from the container to container. The lack of top-down design direction engenders a rich and sometimes messy texture, which creates a vibrant place to live and work. The architecture becomes the backdrop to interactions, conversations, events, and the evolution of creative businesses.

Das Projekt besteht aus 33 gebrauchten Schiffscontainern, die so konfiguriert sind, dass sie auf programmatische und kontextuelle Parameter reagieren. Der sich daraus ergebende Rahmen ermöglicht den individuellen Ausdruck und gleichzeitig die Interaktion mit der Gemeinschaft.

Die Module können neu konfiguriert, entfernt oder verschoben werden, so dass sie in Zukunft verändert und angepasst werden können.

Das Projekt ist mit mehreren Kontexten verbunden, darunter die bestehenden Strukturen, das Containernetz, das sich durch Oakland zieht, und die lokale Gemeinschaft der kreativen Unternehmer. Die zugrundeliegenden Container haben eine Leinwand geschaffen, und eine Gemeinschaft hat das Projekt mit ihren eigenen Änderungen nach ihren eigenen Bedürfnissen bevölkert. Die Ergebnisse sind von einem Container zum anderen sehr unterschiedlich. Das Fehlen einer vertikalen Gestaltungslinie führt zu einer reichen und manchmal chaotischen Textur, die einen lebendigen Ort zum Leben und Arbeiten schafft. Die Architektur wird dann zur Kulisse für Interaktionen, Gespräche, Veranstaltungen und die Entwicklung kreativer Unternehmen.

Le projet se compose de 33 conteneurs d'expédition usagés qui sont configurés pour répondre à des paramètres programmatiques et contextuels. Le cadre qui en résulte permet l'expression individuelle et, simultanément, l'interaction communautaire.

Les modules peuvent être reconfigurés, retirés ou déplacés, ce qui permet des modifications et des adaptations futures.

Le projet est lié à plusieurs contextes, notamment les structures existantes, le réseau de conteneurs qui traverse Oakland et la communauté locale d'entrepreneurs créatifs. Les conteneurs sous-jacents ont créé un canevas, et une communauté a peuplé le projet de ses propres modifications, en fonction de ses propres besoins. Les résultats sont radicalement différents d'un conteneur à l'autre. L'absence d'orientation verticale du design engendre une texture riche et parfois désordonnée, créant un lieu de vie et de travail dynamique. L'architecture devient alors la toile de fond des interactions, des conversations, des événements et de l'évolution des entreprises créatives.

El proyecto consta de 33 contenedores marítimos usados que se configuran para responder a parámetros programáticos y contextuales. El marco resultante permite la expresión individual y, simultáneamente, la interacción comunitaria.

Los módulos tienen el potencial de ser reconfigurados, eliminados o reubicados, lo que permite una futura modificación y adaptación.

El proyecto está conectado a varios contextos que incluyen las estructuras existentes, la red de contenedores que atraviesa Oakland y la comunidad local de empresarios creativos. Los contenedores subyacentes crearon un lienzo, y una comunidad ha poblado el proyecto con sus propias modificaciones, según sus propias necesidades. Los resultados son dramáticamente diferentes de un contenedor a otro. La falta de una dirección de diseño vertical engendra una textura rica y a veces desordenada, que crea un lugar vibrante para vivir y trabajar. La arquitectura se convierte entonces en el telón de fondo de las interacciones, las conversaciones, los eventos y la evolución de las empresas creativas.

PACIFIC
CHARTER
SCHOOL
DEVELOPMENT

ARTHUR MAC'S
TAP & SNACK
COMING - SOON!

XING
SCHOOL
SLOW

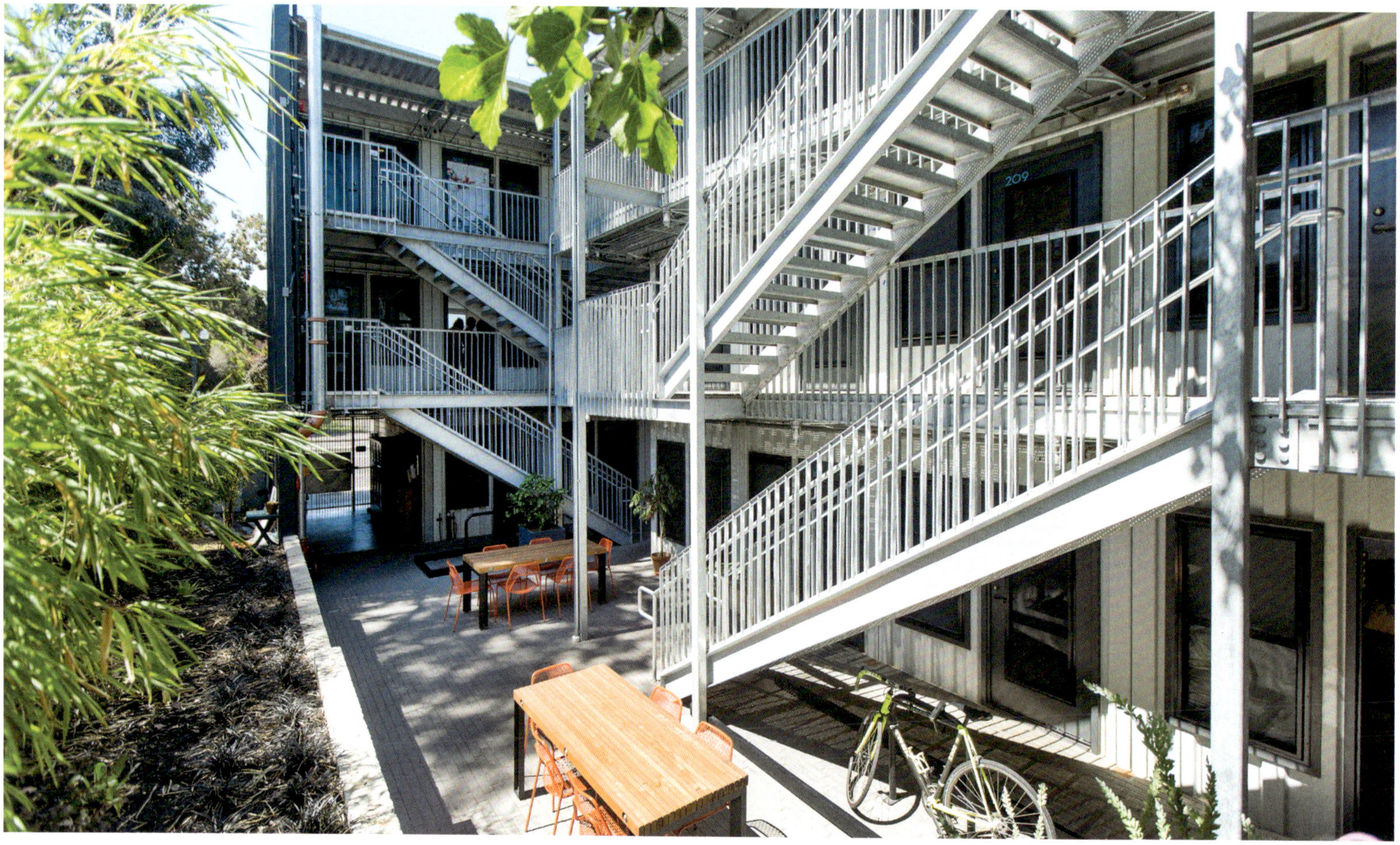

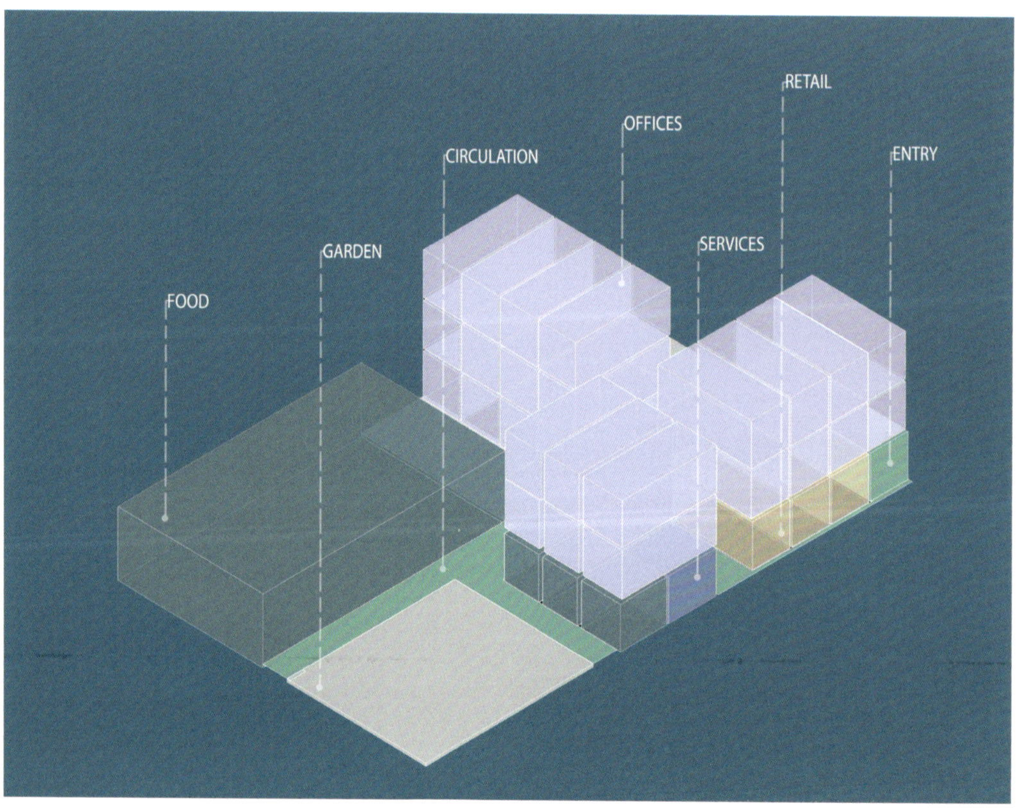

Diagram

LUCID VITALITY
Oakland Printing Co.
CONTACT RECORDS
LA LOBA
FOGGY NOTION

EXIT

EXIT

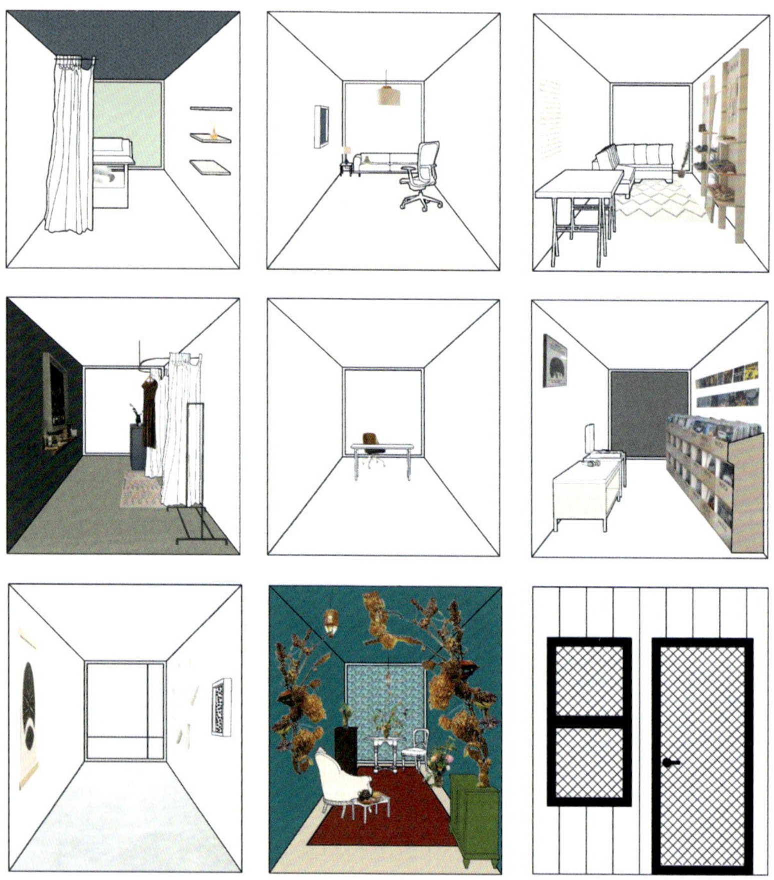

Sketches

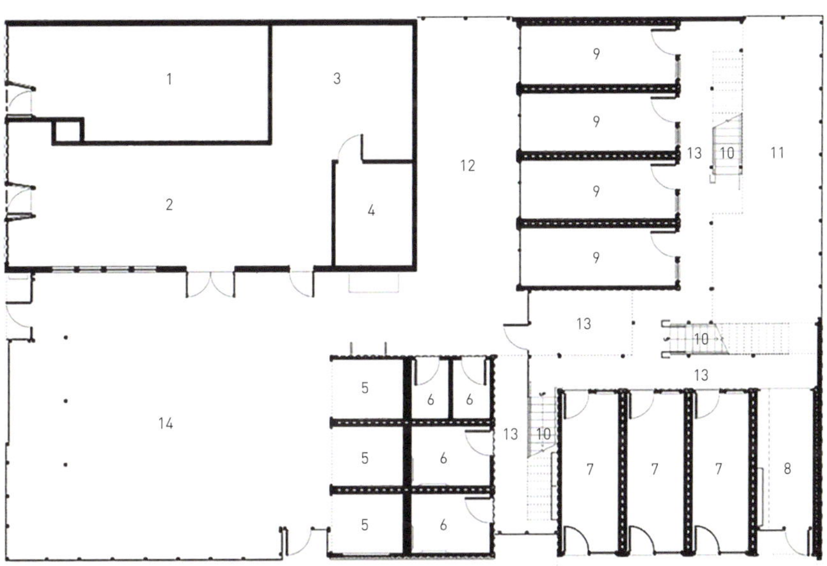

First level

1. Coffee shop
2. Restaurant
3. Restaurant prep area
4. Cold storage
5. Retail room
6. Restroom
7. Retail
8. Utility area
9. Office
10. Stair
11. Back yard
12. Alcove
13. Hallway
14. Seating area

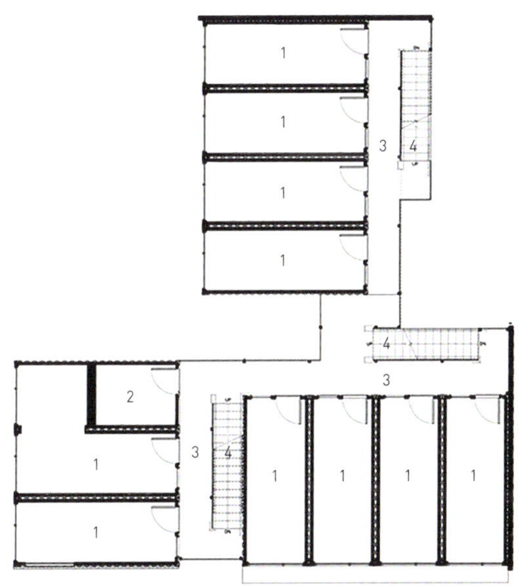

Second level

1. Office
2. Bathroom
3. Hallway
4. Stair

BJB ARCHITECTS

Barry Babikian

BJB Architects is a multi-disciplinary architectural firm with a broad range of experience from small to large scale projects. Operating for over a decade, BJB Architects has delivered numerous successful projects from concept to built form. We believe that a proactive approach to creating functional and well designed spaces is fundamental to the ongoing success and longevity of projects, and at the heart of this is the sound collaboration between ourselves and our clients.

BJB Architects ist ein multidisziplinäres Architekturbüro mit umfassender Erfahrung sowohl in kleinen als auch in großen Projekten. BJB Architects ist seit mehr als einem Jahrzehnt tätig und hat zahlreiche erfolgreiche Projekte vom Konzept bis zur Ausführung realisiert.
Wir sind davon überzeugt, dass ein proaktiver Ansatz zur Schaffung funktionaler und gut gestalteter Räume von grundlegender Bedeutung für den anhaltenden Erfolg und die Langlebigkeit von Projekten ist. Im Mittelpunkt steht dabei die enge Zusammenarbeit zwischen uns und unseren Kunden.

BJB Architects est un cabinet d'architecture pluridisciplinaire qui possède une vaste expérience des projets de petite et grande envergure. En activité depuis plus d'une décennie, BJB Architects a réalisé de nombreux projets réussis, du concept à la forme bâtie.
Nous sommes convaincus qu'une approche proactive de la création d'espaces fonctionnels et bien conçus est fondamentale pour le succès et la longévité des projets, et la collaboration étroite entre nous et nos clients est au cœur de cette démarche.

BJB Architects es un estudio de arquitectura multidisciplinar con una amplia experiencia en proyectos de pequeña y gran envergadura. En funcionamiento desde hace más de una década, BJB Architects ha realizado numerosos proyectos de éxito, desde el concepto hasta la forma construida.
Creemos que un enfoque pro activo para crear espacios funcionales y bien diseñados es fundamental para el éxito continuo y la longevidad de los proyectos, y en el centro de esto está la sólida colaboración entre nosotros y nuestros clientes.

work inc
EM'S NORTHSHORE AUTOMOTIVE
P MOTOR CYCLES ONLY

work inc

BAYS 6-8 HERITAGE OFFICES

Sidney, Australia | Photos: © Mike Chorley Photography

Bays 6-8 sets out to redefine the "shared office" concept, by giving businesses the opportunity to occupy private spaces within a larger collective community.
Located under the northern approach to the Sydney Harbour Bridge and filled with rich heritage, the project embraces the industrial heritage of the site, and incorporates a material palette of concrete, glass and steel shipping containers, in order to find the balance between the cold industrial shell and a warm inviting space people are inspired by.
The industrial heritage has been preserved and enriched through the use of a raw, exposed steel structure and repurposed shipping containers. A strong focus on creating a richly textured and layered building fabric from raw and unfinished materials establishes a benchmark for responsible sustainable architecture.
The adaptive reuse of Bays 6-8 has breathed new life into an otherwise neglected space, whilst minimising resources and the footprint of the project, as well as protecting and showcasing historic value.

Bays 6-8 will das Konzept des „Gemeinschaftsbüros" neu definieren, indem es Unternehmen die Möglichkeit gibt, private Räume innerhalb einer größeren kollektiven Gemeinschaft zu nutzen.
Das Projekt befindet sich unter der nördlichen Zufahrt zur Sydney Harbour Bridge und ist reich an kulturellem Erbe. Es greift das industrielle Erbe des Standorts auf und verwendet eine Materialpalette aus Beton, Glas und Stahl von Schiffscontainern, um ein Gleichgewicht zwischen der kühlen industriellen Hülle und einem warmen, einladenden Raum zu schaffen, der Menschen inspiriert.
Das industrielle Erbe wurde durch die Verwendung einer unbehandelten Stahlstruktur und wiederverwendeter Schiffscontainer bewahrt und aufgewertet. Die besondere Aufmerksamkeit, die der Schaffung einer reich strukturierten und vielschichtigen Bausubstanz aus rohen und unbearbeiteten Materialien gewidmet wird, setzt einen Maßstab für verantwortungsvolle, nachhaltige Architektur.
Die adaptive Umnutzung des Projekts hat einem ansonsten vernachlässigten Raum neues Leben eingehaucht, während gleichzeitig die Ressourcen und der Platzbedarf minimiert und der historische Wert des Gebäudes geschützt und hervorgehoben wurden.

Bays 6-8 vise à redéfinir le concept de « bureau partagé », en donnant aux entreprises la possibilité d'occuper des espaces privés au sein d'une communauté collective plus large.
Situé sous l'approche nord du pont du port de Sydney et riche en patrimoine, le projet embrasse l'héritage industriel du site et incorpore une palette de matériaux en béton, verre et acier de conteneur d'expédition, visant à trouver un équilibre entre l'enveloppe industrielle froide et un espace chaleureux et accueillant qui inspire les gens.
Le patrimoine industriel a été préservé et enrichi grâce à l'utilisation d'une structure en acier non traité et de conteneurs d'expédition réutilisés. L'attention particulière accordée à la création d'un tissu de construction richement texturé et stratifié à partir de matériaux bruts et non finis constitue une référence en matière d'architecture durable et responsable.
La réutilisation adaptative du projet a insufflé une nouvelle vie à un espace autrement négligé, tout en minimisant les ressources et l'empreinte au sol et en protégeant et mettant en valeur sa valeur historique.

Bays 6-8 se propone redefinir el concepto de «oficina compartida», dando a las empresas la oportunidad de ocupar espacios privados dentro de una comunidad colectiva más amplia.
Situado bajo el acceso norte al puente del puerto de Sídney y repleto de rico patrimonio, el proyecto abraza la herencia industrial del lugar e incorpora una paleta de materiales de hormigón, vidrio y acero de contenedores de transporte marítimo, con el fin de encontrar el equilibrio entre la fría envoltura industrial y un espacio cálido y acogedor que inspire a la gente.
El patrimonio industrial se ha conservado y enriquecido mediante el uso de una estructura de acero sin tratar y contenedores de transporte reutilizados. La especial atención prestada a la creación de un tejido constructivo rico en texturas y capas a partir de materiales brutos e inacabados establece un punto de referencia para la arquitectura sostenible responsable.
La re utilización adaptativa del proyecto ha insuflado nueva vida a un espacio de otro modo descuidado, minimizando al mismo tiempo los recursos y la huella y protegiendo y mostrando su valor histórico.

work
inc

work
inc

inc

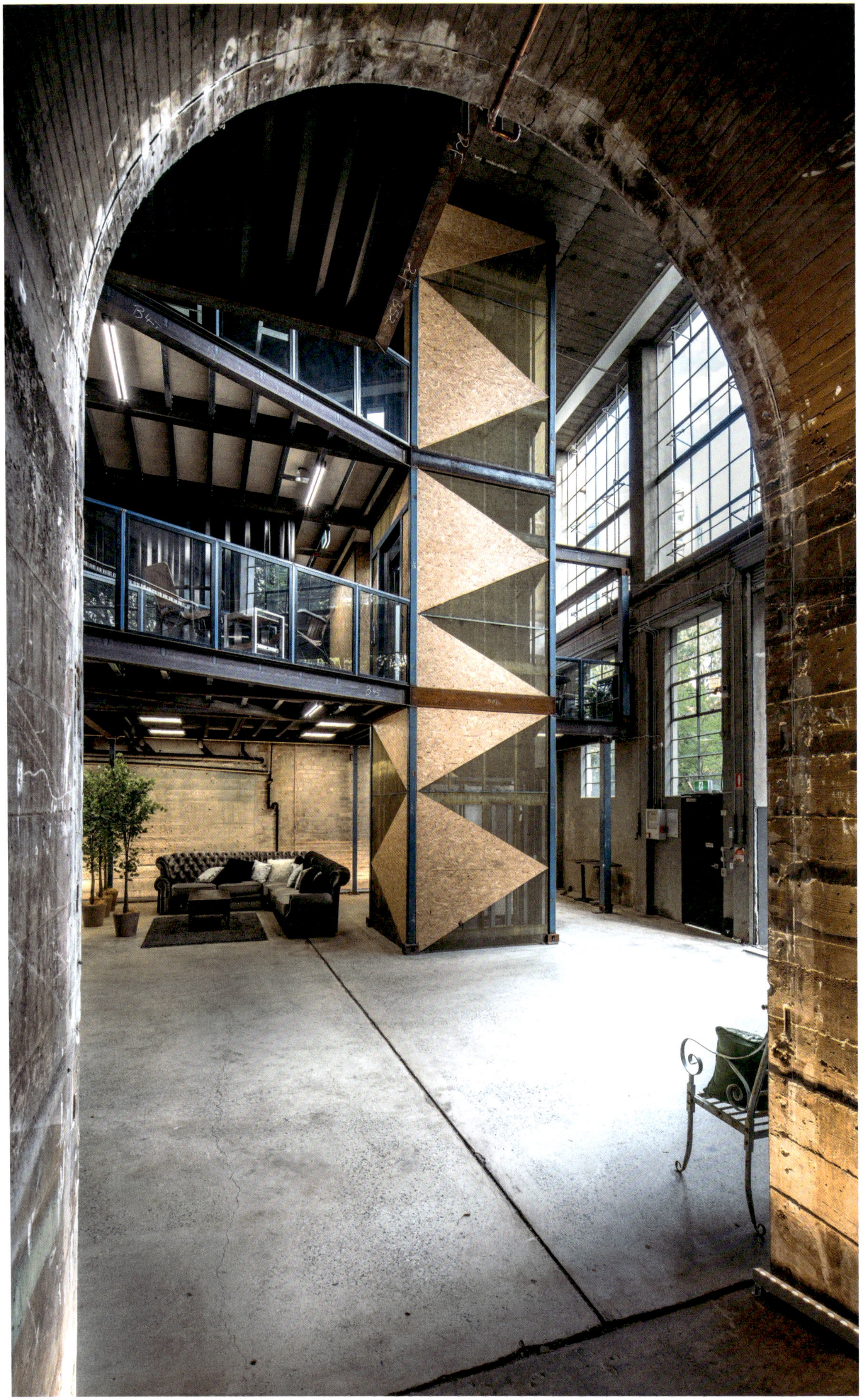

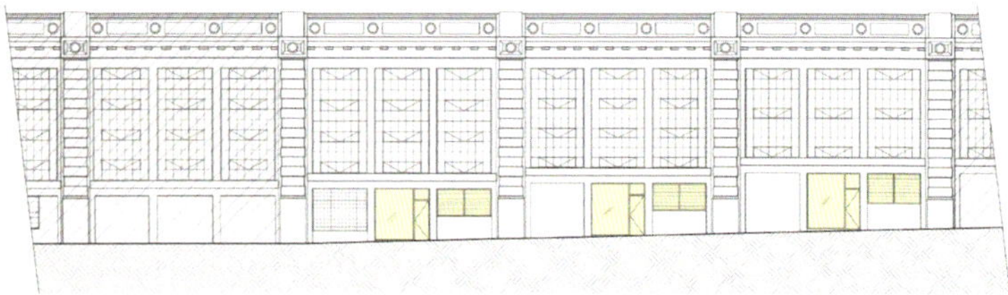

Pacific Highway elevation

Pacific Highway elevation

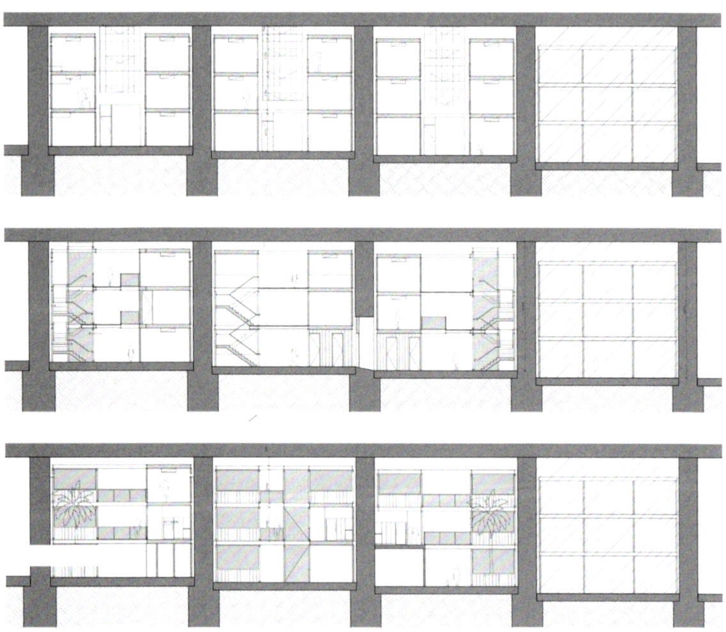

Section 01

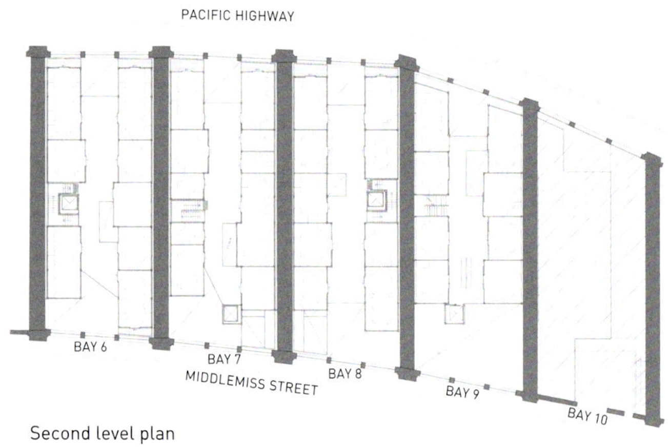

Second level plan

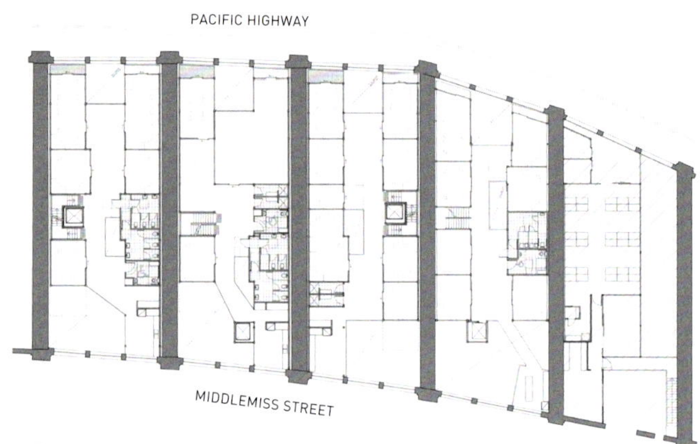

First level plan

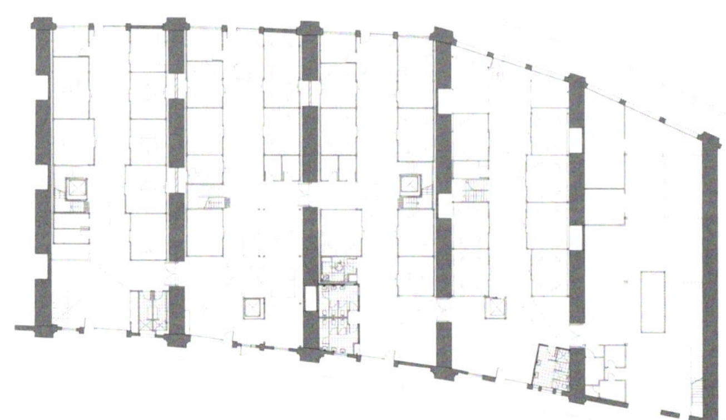

Ground floor plan

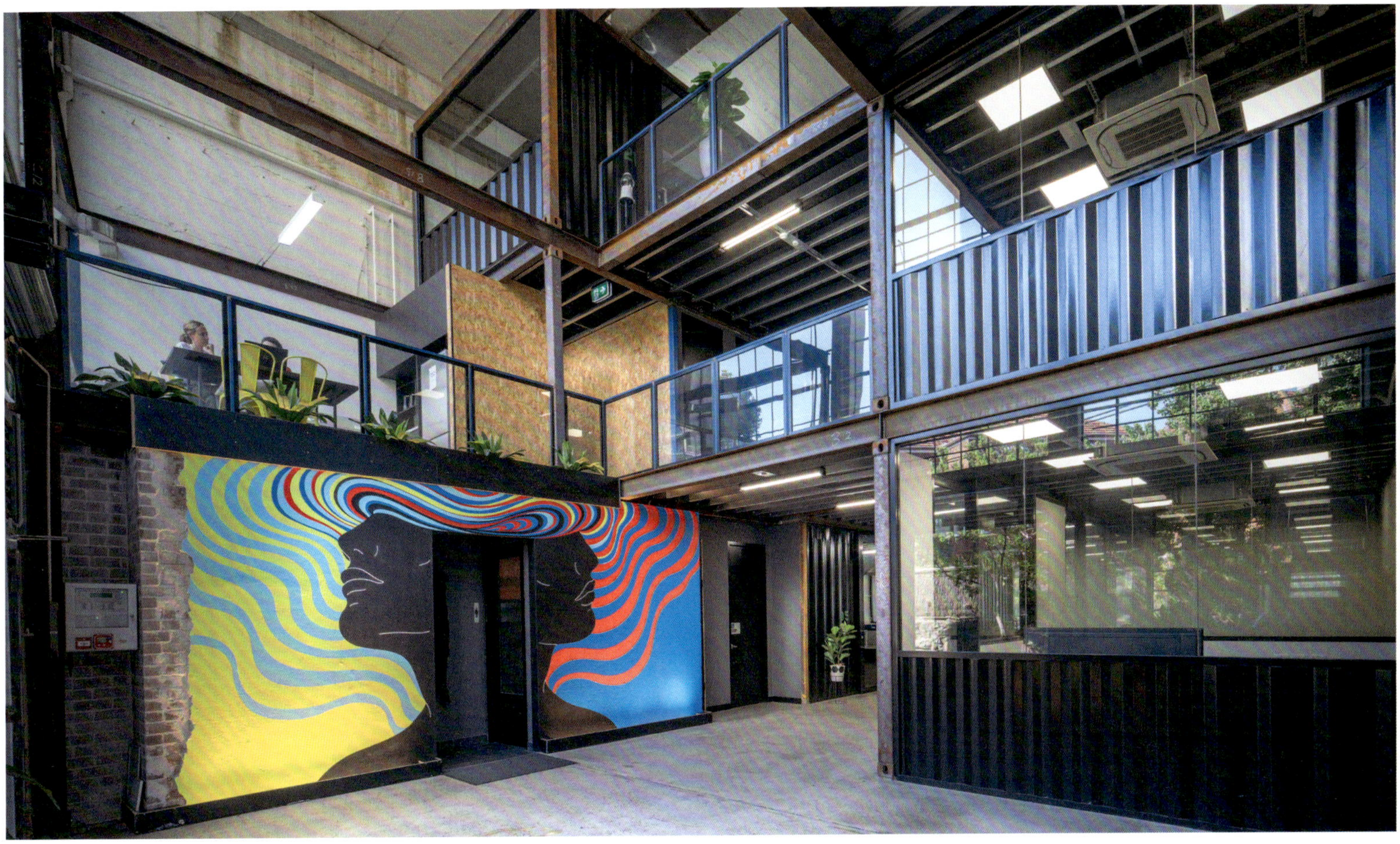

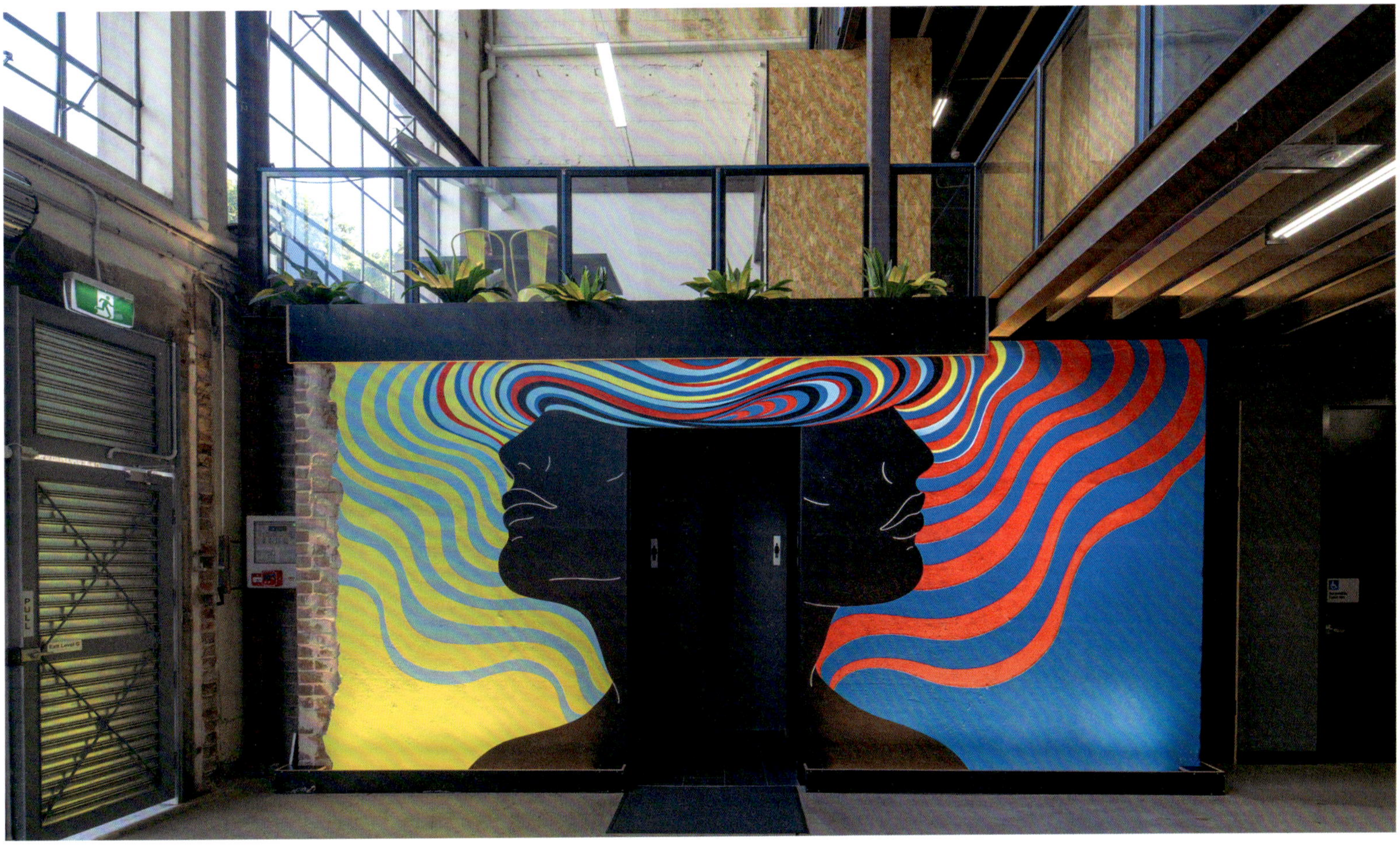

work
inc

CAZA

Carlos Arnaiz

CAZA is a Brooklyn-based design studio and think tank with offices in Manila, Philippines; Bogotá, Colombia; and Lima, Peru that creates concept-driven environments, buildings, and urban plans. We explore how architecture can shape meaningful experiences, enhance its context, connect people to place and heritage, and bring about a more sustainable future.

CAZA ist ein in Brooklyn ansässiges Designstudio und Think Tank mit Büros in Manila (Philippinen), Bogota (Kolumbien) und Lima (Peru), das konzeptgesteuerte Umgebungen, Gebäude und Stadtpläne entwirft. Wir erforschen, wie Architektur sinnvolle Erlebnisse gestalten, ihren Kontext verbessern, Menschen mit Orten und dem kulturellen Erbe verbinden und eine nachhaltigere Zukunft erreichen kann.

CAZA est un studio de design et un groupe de réflexion basé à Brooklyn, avec des bureaux à Manille (Philippines), Bogota (Colombie) et Lima (Pérou), qui crée des environnements, des bâtiments et des plans urbains basés sur des concepts. Nous explorons la manière dont l'architecture peut façonner des expériences significatives, améliorer leur contexte, relier les gens aux lieux et au patrimoine, et assurer un avenir plus durable.

CAZA es un estudio de diseño y un laboratorio de ideas con sede en Brooklyn y oficinas en Manila (Filipinas), Bogotá (Colombia) y Lima (Perú) que crea entornos, edificios y planes urbanos basados en el concepto. Exploramos cómo la arquitectura puede dar forma a experiencias significativas, mejorar su contexto, conectar a la gente con el lugar y el patrimonio, y lograr un futuro más sostenible.

www.cazarch.com

One bedroom

Studio

ACCESSORY DWELLING UNIT (ADU)

Photos: © Spacial Homes

An accessory dwelling unit (ADU) is a smaller, independent dwelling unit located on the same lot as the main residence. ADUs have recently garnered more attention as a potential solution to the affordable housing crisis that leverages existing city infrastructure and prevents urban sprawl. Exploring this idea, CAZA developed two prototype ADUs—a studio unit and a one-bedroom unit—that are both comfortable and cost-effective. Custom-designed elements like murphy beds, wall units, and flexible furniture systems provide ample storage while maximizing usable space. Clerestory windows and sliding glass panels fill the units with natural light. The design minimizes the units' environmental impact, making the ADU type—which typically carries a large carbon footprint—a sustainable housing solution. The prototype is the first ADU to receive an Energy Star rating. Rooftop solar panels generate energy to power the unit, strategically located windows maximize cross-ventilation, and the exterior walls support plantings. Sliding glass panels allow residents to open the house directly to a deck or garden, creating indoor-outdoor living environments.

Eine Zubehör-Wohneinheit (ADU) ist eine kleinere, freistehende Wohneinheit, die sich auf demselben Grundstück wie der Hauptwohnsitz befindet. In letzter Zeit haben ADUs als mögliche Lösung für die Krise des bezahlbaren Wohnraums, die die vorhandene städtische Infrastruktur nutzt und eine Zersiedelung der Landschaft verhindert, mehr Aufmerksamkeit erhalten. Um diese Idee zu erforschen, hat CAZA zwei ADU-Prototypen entwickelt - ein Studio und eine Ein-Zimmer-Einheit - die sowohl komfortabel als auch kostengünstig sind. Maßgefertigte Elemente wie Schrankbetten, Wandschränke und flexible Möbelsysteme bieten reichlich Stauraum und maximieren die Nutzfläche. Große Fenster und Glasschiebetüren versorgen die Wohnungen mit natürlichem Licht. Das Design minimiert die Auswirkungen auf die Umwelt und macht den ADU-Typ, der normalerweise einen großen Kohlenstoff-Fußabdruck hat, zu einer nachhaltigen Wohnlösung. Der Prototyp ist das erste ADU, das mit dem Energy Star ausgezeichnet wurde. Die Solarpaneele auf dem Dach erzeugen Energie für den Raum, strategisch platzierte Fenster maximieren die Querlüftung und die Außenwände sind für die Bepflanzung vorbereitet. Mit Hilfe von Glasschiebeelementen können die Bewohner das Haus direkt zu einer Terrasse oder einem Garten hin öffnen und so Innen- und Außenwohnbereiche schaffen.

Un logement accessoire (ADU) est un logement plus petit, détaché, situé sur le même terrain que la résidence principale. Récemment, les ADU ont fait l'objet d'une attention accrue en tant que solution possible à la crise du logement abordable, en tirant parti des infrastructures urbaines existantes et en évitant l'étalement urbain. Pour explorer cette idée, CAZA a développé deux prototypes d'ADU - un studio et une unité d'une chambre à coucher - qui sont à la fois confortables et rentables. Des éléments conçus sur mesure, tels que des lits Murphy, des unités murales et des systèmes d'ameublement flexibles, offrent un grand espace de rangement tout en maximisant l'espace utilisable. De grandes fenêtres et des panneaux coulissants en verre remplissent les unités de lumière naturelle. La conception minimise l'impact sur l'environnement, ce qui fait du type ADU - qui a généralement une forte empreinte carbone - une solution de logement durable. Le prototype est le premier ADU à recevoir un classement Energy Star. Des panneaux solaires installés sur le toit produisent de l'énergie pour alimenter l'espace, des fenêtres stratégiquement placées maximisent la ventilation croisée et les murs extérieurs sont préparés pour la plantation. Des panneaux de verre coulissants permettent aux résidents d'ouvrir la maison directement sur une terrasse ou un jardin, créant ainsi des environnements de vie intérieurs/extérieurs.

Una unidad de vivienda accesoria (ADU) es una unidad de vivienda más pequeña e independiente situada en la misma parcela que la residencia principal. Recientemente, las ADU han recibido más atención como una posible solución a la crisis de la vivienda asequible que aprovecha la infraestructura existente en la ciudad y evita la expansión urbana. Para explorar esta idea, CAZA ha desarrollado dos prototipos de ADU —un estudio y una unidad de un dormitorio— que son cómodos y rentables. Los elementos diseñados a medida, como las camas Murphy, las unidades de pared y los sistemas de mobiliario flexible, proporcionan un amplio almacenamiento al tiempo que maximizan el espacio útil. Los ventanales y los paneles deslizantes de cristal llenan las unidades de luz natural. El diseño minimiza el impacto medioambiental, lo que hace que el tipo de ADU —que normalmente conlleva una gran huella de carbono— sea una solución de vivienda sostenible. El prototipo es la primera ADU que recibe la calificación Energy Star. Los paneles solares de la azotea generan energía para alimentar el espacio, las ventanas estratégicamente situadas maximizan la ventilación cruzada y las paredes exteriores están preparadas para ser plantadas. Los paneles deslizantes de cristal permiten a los residentes abrir la casa directamente a una terraza o a un jardín, creando entornos de vida interiores y exteriores.

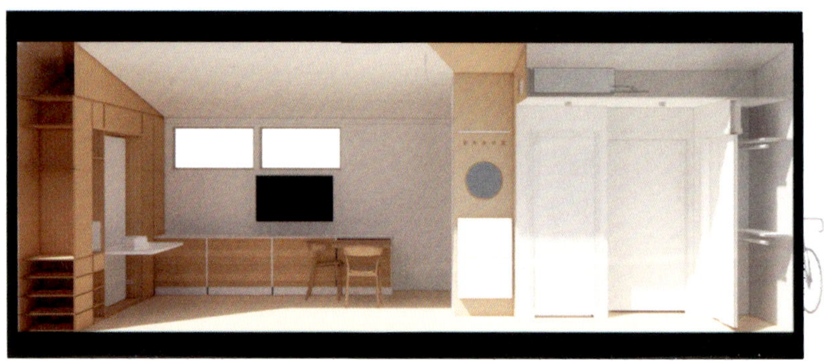

Studio section

One bed section

DINAMO STUDIO

Erick Ledezma Fernández

Construction Technician from the University of Costa Rica, 1992 and Bachelor of Architecture from the Central University, 2004. In 2008 he created Dinamo Studio together with Architect Marco Avila. He has participated in the Biennials of the College of Architects of Costa Rica, receiving Honorable Mention of the Metalco Grand Prize in 2006.

His objective when designing is that the sum of a practical architecture and an efficient construction process, result in a functional, stable, aesthetic and sustainable project, capable of adapting to the expectations of the inhabitant and its environment.

Bautechniker an der Universität von Costa Rica, 1992, und Bachelor in Architektur an der Zentraluniversität, 2004. Im Jahr 2008 gründete er zusammen mit dem Architekten Marco Avila das Studio Dinamo. Er hat an den Biennalen des Architektenkollegiums von Costa Rica teilgenommen und erhielt 2006 eine lobende Erwähnung für den Großen Preis von Metalco.

Sein Ziel bei der Planung ist es, dass die Summe einer praktischen Architektur und eines effizienten Bauprozesses ein funktionales, stabiles, ästhetisches und nachhaltiges Projekt ergibt, das sich den Erwartungen der Bewohner und der Umgebung anpasst.

Technicien en construction de l'université du Costa Rica, 1992 et licence en architecture de l'université centrale, 2004. En 2008, il a créé Dinamo Studio avec l'architecte Marco Avila. Il a participé aux biennales du Collège des architectes du Costa Rica, recevant la mention honorable du grand prix Metalco en 2006.

Son objectif lors de la conception est que la somme d'une architecture pratique et d'un processus de construction efficace, aboutisse à un projet fonctionnel, stable, esthétique et durable, capable de s'adapter aux attentes de l'habitant et de son environnement.

Técnico en Construcción por la Universidad de Costa Rica, 1992 y Licenciado en Arquitectura por la Universidad Central, 2004. En 2008 crea Dinamo Studio en conjunto con el Arquitecto Marco Avila. Ha participado en las Bienales del Colegio de Arquitectos de Costa Rica, recibiendo Mención de Honor del Gran Premio Metalco en el año 2006.

Su objetivo al diseñar es que la suma de una arquitectura práctica y un proceso de construcción eficiente, den como resultado un proyecto funcional, estable, estético y sostenible, capaz de adecuarse a las expectativas del habitante y a su entorno.

OFICINAS F5.6 / FULFIERROS

San José, Costa Rica | Photos: © Roberto D'Ambrosio

The project consists of 8 containers in total, 5 of 40 feet and 3 of 20 feet, which house the work units, reception, production and new business, meeting room, editing, kitchen, dining room and bathrooms, administration and archive, animation, editing, audio booth, a cantilevered container with roof on the main facade serves as a space for rest. At the assembly level, some containers are isolated, others are superimposed on each other, and others are juxtaposed creating volumes and voids and double-height spaces, the connecting spaces are platforms used as play areas. The external enclosures and the roof are built with Total Span type thermopanel, a material that provides thermal-acoustic insulation and is very well associated with the image of the container due to its ribbed tray-type finish. Each tray of the thermopanel sheet was used on the façades to achieve a chromatic composition of vertical stripes with gradient shades of green, grey and blue. In the end, all these modulated components, easy to assemble on site, became a typological alternative that helped us to resolve a complex architectural program for this group of audiovisual production professionals.

Das Projekt besteht aus insgesamt 8 Containern, 5 von 40 Fuß und 3 von 20 Fuß, in denen die Arbeitseinheiten, Empfang, Produktion und Neugeschäft, Besprechungsraum, Redaktion, Küche, Speisesaal und Sanitäranlagen, Verwaltung und Archiv, Animation, Schnitt, Audiokabine untergebracht sind, ein auskragender Container mit Dach an der Hauptfassade dient als Raum zum Ausruhen. Auf der Montageebene sind einige Container isoliert, andere übereinander und wieder andere nebeneinander angeordnet, wodurch Volumina und Leerräume sowie Räume mit doppelter Höhe entstehen; die Verbindungsräume sind Plattformen, die als Spielbereiche genutzt werden. Die Außenverkleidungen und das Dach bestehen aus Thermopaneelen des Typs Total Span, einem Material, das eine thermische und akustische Isolierung bietet und aufgrund seiner gerippten, schalenartigen Oberfläche sehr gut mit dem Image des Containers assoziiert wird. Jede Schale der Thermopanel-Platte wurde an den Fassaden verwendet, um eine chromatische Komposition aus vertikalen Streifen mit Farbverläufen in Grün, Grau und Blau zu erzielen. Letztendlich wurden all diese modulierten Komponenten, die vor Ort leicht zu montieren sind, zu einer typologischen Alternative, die uns half, ein komplexes architektonisches Programm für diese Gruppe von Fachleuten für audiovisuelle Produktion zu lösen.

Le projet se compose de 8 conteneurs au total, 5 de 40 pieds et 3 de 20 pieds, qui abritent les unités de travail, la réception, la production et les nouvelles affaires, la salle de réunion, le montage, la cuisine, la salle à manger et les salles de bain, l'administration et les archives, l'animation, le montage, la cabine audio, un conteneur en porte-à-faux avec un toit sur la façade principale sert d'espace de repos, plus une future cafétéria a été prévue au rez-de-chaussée dans le parking. Au niveau de l'assemblage, certains conteneurs sont isolés, d'autres sont superposés les uns aux autres, d'autres encore sont juxtaposés créant des volumes et des vides et des espaces à double hauteur, les espaces de liaison sont des plates-formes utilisées comme aires de jeux. Les enveloppes extérieures et le toit sont construits en thermopanneau de type Total Span, un matériau qui assure une isolation thermique et acoustique e t qui est très bien associé à l'image du conteneur grâce à sa finition de type plateau nervuré. Chaque plateau de la feuille thermopanel a été utilisé sur les façades pour réaliser une composition chromatique de bandes verticales avec des dégradés de vert, gris et bleu. En définitive, tous ces composants modulés, faciles à assembler sur place, sont devenus une alternative typologique qui nous a aidés à résoudre un programme architectural complexe pour ce groupe de professionnels de la production audiovisuelle.

El proyecto se compone de 8 contenedores en total, 5 de 40 pies y 3 de 20 pies, que albergan las unidades de trabajo, recepción, producción y nuevos negocios, sala de reuniones, edición, cocina, comedor y baños, administración y archivo, animación, edición, cabina de audio, un contenedor en voladizo con azotea en la fachada principal sirve de espacio para el descanso. A nivel de montaje, unos contenedores están aislados, otros están sobrepuestos entre sí, y otros se yuxtaponen creando volúmenes y vacíos y espacios a doble altura, los espacios conectores son plataformas que se usan como zonas de juegos. Los cerramientos externos y la cubierta están construidos con termopanel tipo Total Span, material que aporta aislamiento termo-acústico y se asocia muy bien a la imagen del contenedor por su acabado acanalado tipo bandeja. Cada bandeja de la lámina de termopanel se utilizó en las fachadas para conseguir una composición cromática de franjas verticales con tonos degradados del verde, gris y azul. Al final, todos estos componentes modulados, de fácil ensamblaje sobre el terreno, se convirtieron en una alternativa tipológica que nos ayudó a resolver un complejo programa arquitectónico para este colectivo de profesionales en producción audiovisual.

West elevation

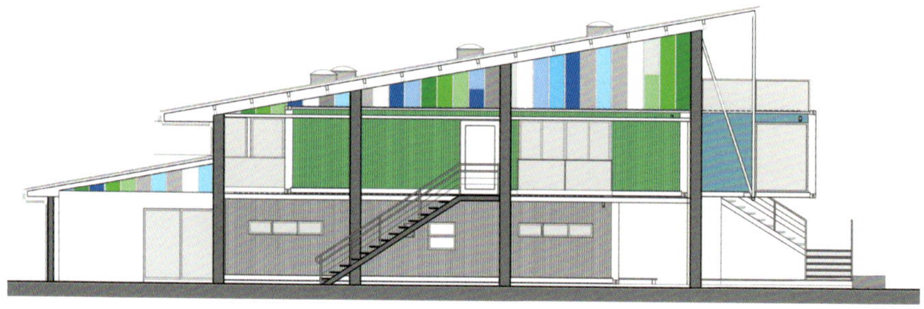

North elevation

West elevation

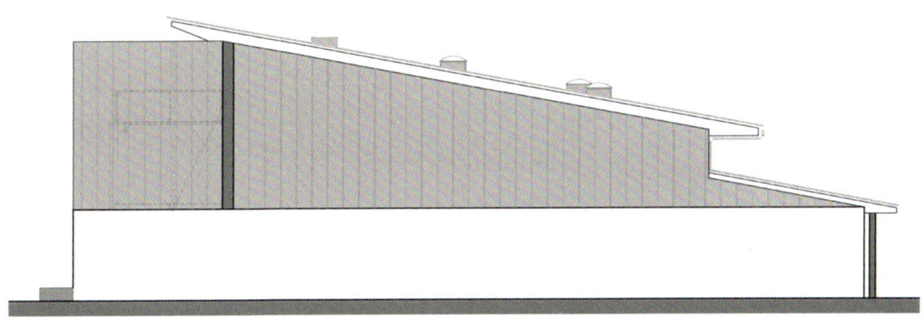

South elevation

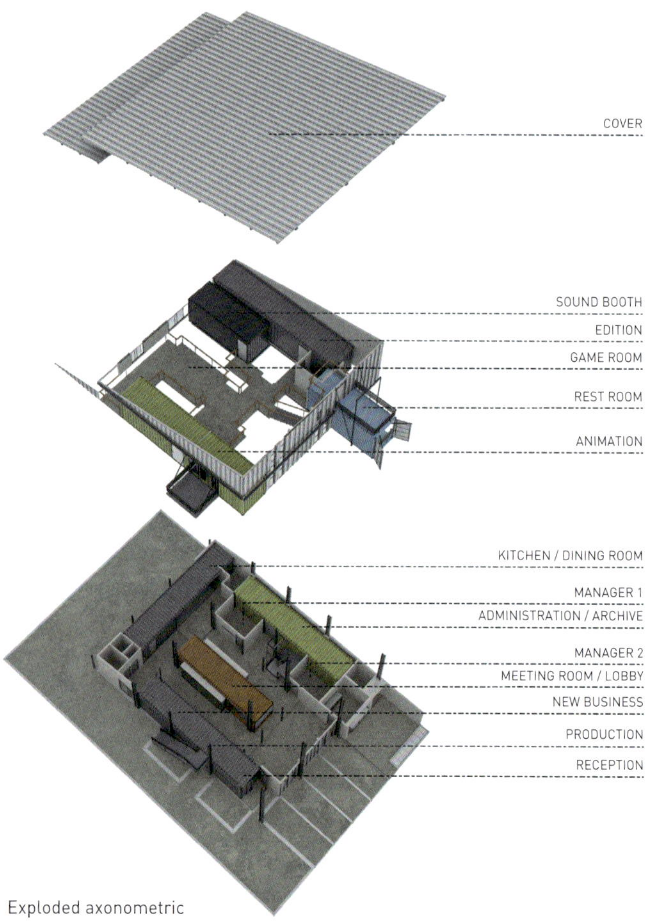

Exploded axonometric

Ground floor plan

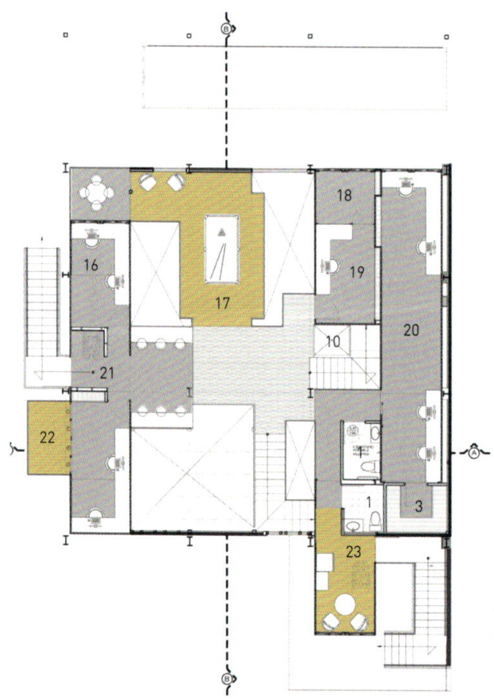

First floor plan

1. Bathroom
2. Kitchen
3. Warehouse
4. Private bathroom
5. New business
6. Meeting room
7. Director
8. Archive
9. Producer
10. Lift
11. Cafeteria
12. Car park
13. Training
14. Administrator
15. Reception
16. Animation
17. Games room
18. Booth
19. Audio
20. Editing
21. Exit
22. Balcony
23. Rest room

Ecotech Design is a full-service architectural practice currently exploring the symbiotic relationships between ecological and technological systems, combined with the integration of natural daylight, ventilation and passive solar energy components to create a *sense of place* that is both inspirational and functional; ie *hybrid container architecture*.

As an architect, Walter Scott Perry has designed, managed and supervised construction of small and large scale residential, commercial, institutional and experimental projects throughout the U.S. for many years.

Ecotech Design ist ein Architekturbüro mit umfassendem Service, das derzeit symbiotische Beziehungen zwischen ökologischen und technologischen Systemen erforscht, kombiniert mit der Integration von natürlichem Licht, Belüftung und passiven Solarenergiekomponenten, um ein Gefühl von Ort zu schaffen, das sowohl inspirierend als auch funktional ist; d.h. hybride Containerarchitektur.

Als Architekt hat Walter Scott Perry viele Jahre damit verbracht, kleine und große Wohn-, Geschäfts-, institutionelle und experimentelle Projekte in den Vereinigten Staaten zu entwerfen, zu leiten und zu überwachen.

Ecotech Design est un cabinet d'architecture à service complet qui explore actuellement les relations symbiotiques entre les systèmes écologiques et technologiques, combinées à l'intégration de la lumière naturelle, de la ventilation et des composants de l'énergie solaire passive afin de créer un sentiment de lieu à la fois inspirant et fonctionnel, c'est-à-dire une architecture hybride de conteneurs.

En tant qu'architecte, Walter Scott Perry a passé de nombreuses années à concevoir, diriger et superviser la construction de projets résidentiels, commerciaux, institutionnel et expérimentaux de petite et grande envergure à travers les États-Unis.

Ecotech Design es un estudio de arquitectura de servicios integrales que actualmente explora las relaciones simbióticas entre los sistemas ecológicos y tecnológicos, combinados con la integración de la luz natural, la ventilación y los componentes de energía solar pasiva para crear un sentido del lugar que sea a la vez inspirador y funcional; es decir, arquitectura híbrida de contenedores.

Como arquitecto, Walter Scott Perry lleva muchos años diseñando, dirigiendo y supervisando la construcción de proyectos residenciales, comerciales, institucionales y experimentales a pequeña y gran escala en todo Estados Unidos.

www. ecotechdesign.com

GENESEO INN

Paso Robles, CA, United States | Photos: © HANA, Paul Vu Photographer. Renders: James Choe

Geneseo Inn represents the third generation of hybrid container architecture by Ecotech Design, one that integrates shipping containers with conventional construction systems in order to address basic space planning issues in residential projects, while demonstrating a creative and dynamic integration of recycled materials within 'pre-engineered' shipping containers originally designed for the global transportation of materials.

The site is a 145 acre winery, Cass Winery located in central, coastal California near Paso Robles. The project consists of (8) BnB units, covered parking and outdoor dining for guests from around the world. The units are arranged in 3 clusters around an existing 60' h. live oak and are constructed of 20' l. and 40' l. shipping containers integrated with conventionally-built 12' h. clerestory spaces that introduce natural daylight and ventilation from above the units. In addition, the "cathedral" ceilings are placed between adjacent 9'6" h. shipping containers to create a dramatic, light-filled interior, as well enhance the views of the surrounding vineyards and valley.

Das Geneseo Inn stellt die dritte Generation der hybriden Containerarchitektur von Ecotech Design dar, bei der Schiffscontainer mit konventionellen Bausystemen kombiniert werden, um grundlegende Raumplanungsprobleme bei Wohnprojekten zu lösen. Gleichzeitig wird eine kreative und dynamische Integration von recycelten Materialien in Schiffscontainer demonstriert, die ursprünglich für den globalen Transport von Materialien „vorgefertigt" wurden.

Das 145 Hektar große Weingut Cass Winery liegt an der zentralen Küste Kaliforniens in der Nähe von Paso Robles. Das Projekt besteht aus (8) BnB-Einheiten, überdachten Parkplätzen und Restaurants im Freien für Gäste aus aller Welt. Die Einheiten sind in drei Gruppen um eine bestehende 60 Fuß hohe Eiche herum angeordnet und bestehen aus 20 Fuß und 40 Fuß langen Containern, die mit konventionellen 12 Fuß hohen Oberlichtern ausgestattet sind, die für natürliches Licht und Belüftung über den Einheiten sorgen. Darüber hinaus wurden „kathedralenartige" Decken zwischen benachbarten 9'6" hohen Containern angebracht, um einen dramatischen, lichtdurchfluteten Innenraum zu schaffen und die Aussicht auf die umliegenden Weinberge und das Tal zu verbessern.

Geneseo Inn représente la troisième génération d'architecture hybride de conteneurs d'Ecotech Design, qui intègre les conteneurs d'expédition aux systèmes de construction conventionnels pour résoudre les problèmes de base de l'aménagement de l'espace dans les projets résidentiels, tout en démontrant une intégration créative et dynamique de matériaux recyclés dans des conteneurs d'expédition initialement « pré-étudiés » pour le transport mondial de matériaux.

Il s'agit d'un domaine viticole de 145 acres, Cass Winery, situé sur la côte centrale de la Californie, près de Paso Robles. Le projet comprend 8 unités BnB, un parking couvert et un restaurant en plein air pour des hôtes du monde entier. Les unités sont disposées en trois groupes autour d'un chêne existant de 60 pieds de haut et sont constituées de conteneurs de 20 et 40 pieds de long intégrés à des puits de lumière conventionnels de 12 pieds de haut qui introduisent la lumière naturelle et la ventilation au-dessus des unités. En outre, des plafonds « cathédrales » sont placés entre des conteneurs adjacents de 9'6" de haut afin de créer un intérieur spectaculaire et lumineux et d'améliorer la vue sur les vignobles et la vallée environnants.

Geneseo Inn representa la tercera generación de arquitectura híbrida de contenedores de Ecotech Design, que integra contenedores marítimos con sistemas de construcción convencionales para resolver problemas básicos de planificación del espacio en proyectos residenciales, al tiempo que demuestra una integración creativa y dinámica de materiales reciclados en contenedores marítimos «pre diseñados» originalmente para el transporte global de materiales.

Se trata de una bodega de 145 acres, Cass Winery, situada en la costa central de California, cerca de Paso Robles. El proyecto consta de (8) unidades BnB, aparcamiento cubierto y comedor al aire libre para huéspedes de todo el mundo. Las unidades están dispuestas en tres grupos en torno a un roble existente de 60 pies de altura y están construidas con contenedores de 20 y 40 pies de longitud integrados con claraboyas convencionales de 12 pies de altura que introducen luz natural y ventilación por encima de las unidades. Además, los techos «catedral» están colocados entre contenedores adyacentes de 9'6" de altura para crear un interior espectacular y lleno de luz, así como para realzar las vistas de los viñedos y el valle circundantes.

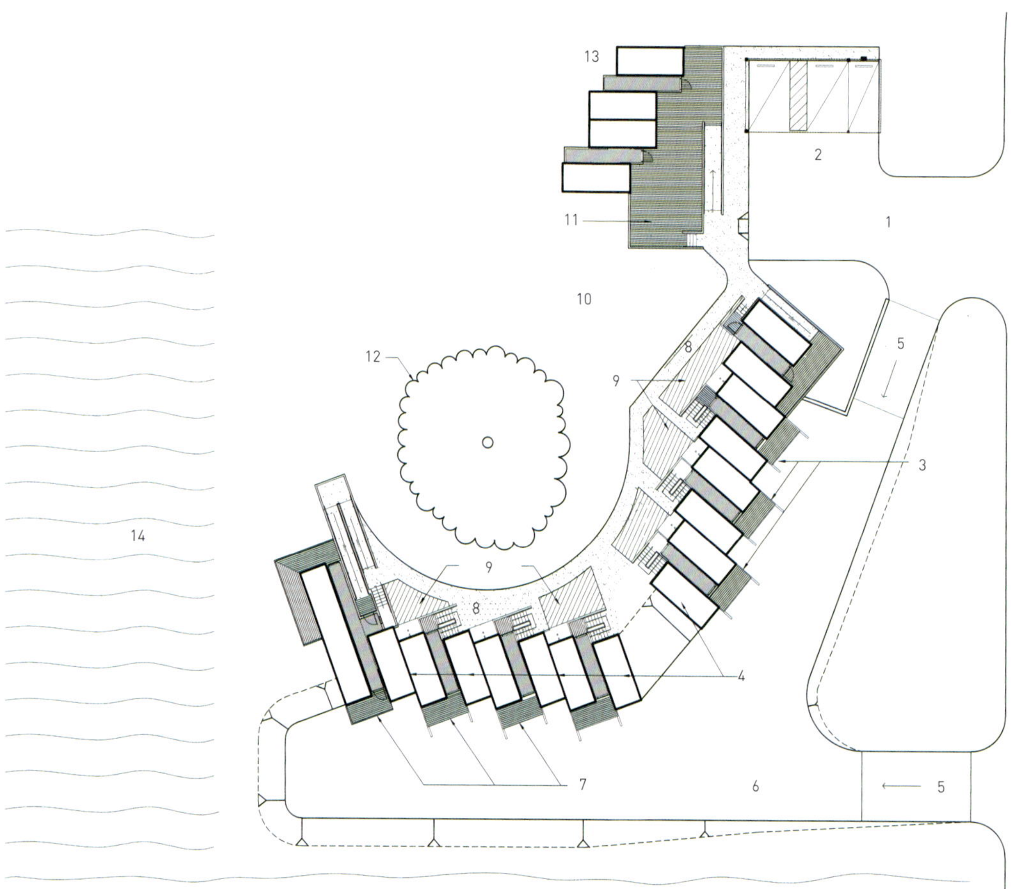

1. Access Road
2. Visitor parking
3. BNB parking under
4. BNB Units
5. Ramp
6. Driveway
7. Decks
8. Walkway
9. Landscaping
10. BBQ
11. Breakfast deck
12. Oak tree
13. Office
14. Vineyard

Site plan

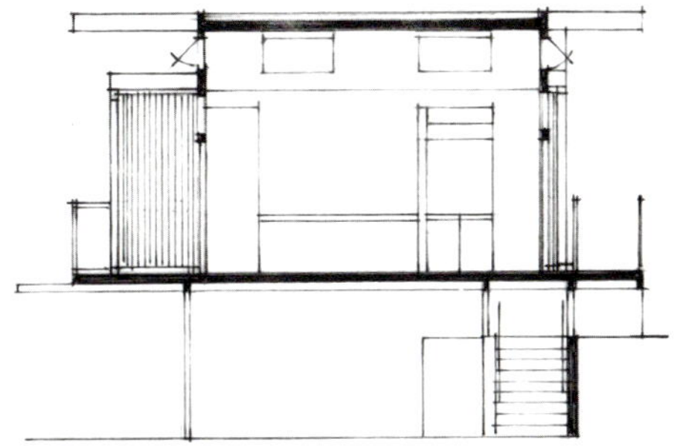

Cross section A

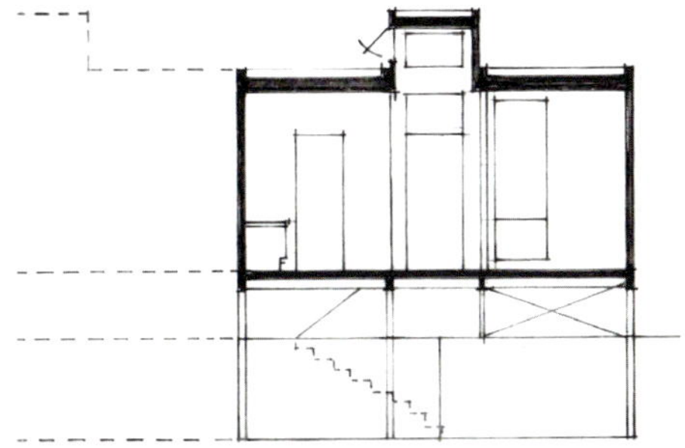

Cross section B

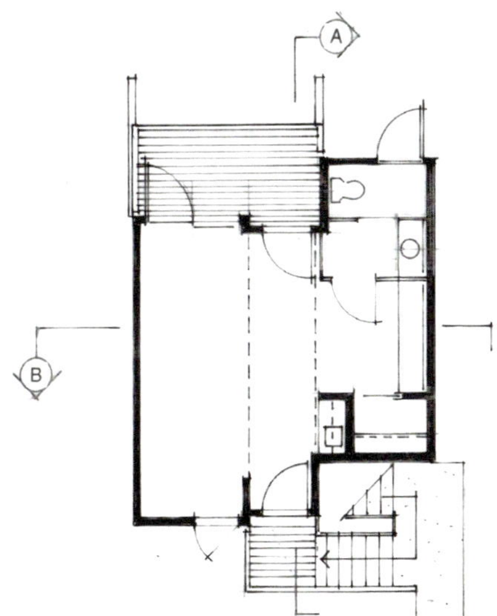

Floor plan

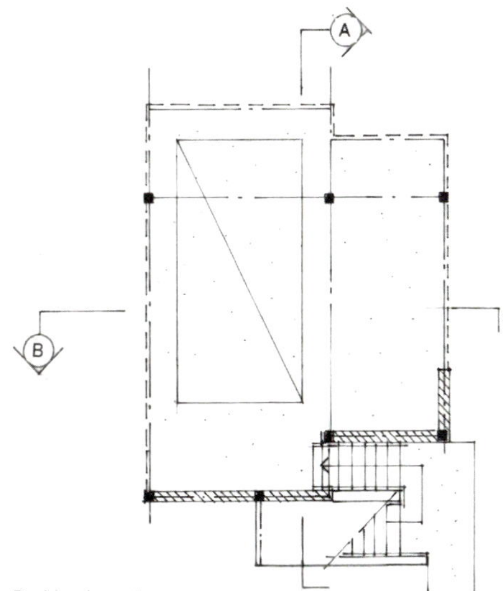

Parking layout

PALEN STUDIO

Joshua Tree, California, United States | Photos: © Jack Parsons, Jack Parsons Photography

Palen Studio at Shadow Mountain is a first generation hybrid container architecture by Ecotech Design that incorporated and integrated shipping containers with conventional construction and pre-engineered steel buildings.

The client, an L.A. film executive and videographer wanted to build a sustainable, contemporary home and studio next to a mountain on a hot, windy desert site at 760 m elevation and several miles from a major earthquake fault. Construction had to be cost-effective, durable, and maintenance-free, being located in the most extreme climate zone in California.

Therefore, the best material for the project was steel. In addition, the lack of a local, competitive construction trade industry made off-site, prefab construction practical and with the close proximity of the ports of L.A. and Long Beach and a surplus of recycled, shipping containers created an obvious and exciting design opportunity. In addition, shipping containers are found throughout the Mojave Desert, are used in many applications and make their adaptation for a residence a thoughtful application of the 1970's term 'appropriate technology'. This project was the first permitted container residence built in San Bernardino County.

Das Palen Studio at Shadow Mountain ist eine hybride Containerarchitektur der ersten Generation von Ecotech Design, bei der Schiffscontainer mit konventionellen Gebäuden und vorgefertigten Stahlgebäuden kombiniert wurden.

Der Bauherr, ein in Los Angeles ansässiger Filmemacher und Videofilmer, wollte ein nachhaltiges, modernes Wohnhaus und Studio an einem Berghang in einer heißen, windigen Wüstengegend, 760 m über dem Meeresspiegel und mehrere Kilometer von einer großen Erdbebenverwerfungslinie entfernt, bauen. Die Konstruktion musste kostengünstig, langlebig und wartungsfrei sein, da sie sich in der extremsten Klimazone Kaliforniens befindet.

Stahl war daher das beste Material für das Projekt. Darüber hinaus machte das Fehlen einer wettbewerbsfähigen lokalen Bauindustrie die Fertigbauweise außerhalb der Baustelle praktisch, und mit der Nähe zu den Häfen von Los Angeles und Long Beach und einem Überschuss an recycelten Schiffscontainern ergab sich eine offensichtliche und spannende Gestaltungsmöglichkeit. Andererseits sind Schiffscontainer überall in der Mojave-Wüste zu finden, werden in vielen Bereichen eingesetzt und machen ihre Anpassung für ein Wohnhaus zu einer durchdachten Anwendung des Begriffs „angemessene Technologie" aus den 1970er Jahren. Dieses Projekt war das erste zugelassene Containerwohnheim, das in San Bernardino County gebaut wurde.

Le Palen Studio at Shadow Mountain est une architecture hybride de conteneurs de première génération réalisée par Ecotech Design qui a incorporé et intégré des conteneurs d'expédition à des bâtiments conventionnels et à des bâtiments en acier préfabriqués.

Le client, un producteur de films et vidéaste basé à Los Angeles, souhaitait construire une maison et un studio durables et contemporains à flanc de montagne, dans un endroit chaud et venteux, situé dans le désert, à 760 mètres d'altitude et à plusieurs kilomètres d'une importante faille sismique. La construction devait être rentable, durable et sans entretien, étant située dans la zone climatique la plus extrême de Californie.

L'acier était donc le meilleur matériau pour le projet. En outre, l'absence d'une industrie locale de la construction compétitive a rendu pratique la construction préfabriquée hors site et, avec la proximité des ports de Los Angeles et de Long Beach et un surplus de conteneurs d'expédition recyclés, une opportunité de conception évidente et passionnante a été créée. D'autre part, on trouve des conteneurs de transport dans tout le désert de Mojave, ils sont utilisés dans de nombreuses applications et leur adaptation à une résidence est une application réfléchie du terme « technologie appropriée » des années 1970. Ce projet a été la première résidence en conteneur autorisée à être construite dans le comté de San Bernardino.

Palen Studio en Shadow Mountain es una arquitectura híbrida de contenedores de primera generación realizada por Ecotech Design que incorporó e integró contenedores de transporte con construcciones convencionales y edificios de acero pre diseñados.

El cliente, un ejecutivo del mundo del cine y videógrafo de Los Ángeles, quería construir una casa y un estudio sostenibles y contemporáneos junto a una montaña, en un lugar desértico, caluroso y ventoso, a 760 m de altitud y a varios kilómetros de una importante falla sísmica. La construcción tenía que ser rentable, duradera y sin mantenimiento, al estar situada en la zona climática más extrema de California.

Por ello, el mejor material para el proyecto era el acero. Además, la falta de una industria de la construcción local competitiva hacía que la construcción prefabricada fuera de las obras fuera práctica y, con la proximidad de los puertos de Los Ángeles y Long Beach y un excedente de contenedores de transporte reciclados, se creó una oportunidad obvia de diseño, ademas de emocionante. Por otro lado, los contenedores de transporte se encuentran en todo el desierto de Mojave, se utilizan en muchas aplicaciones y hacen de su adaptación para una residencia una aplicación reflexiva del término del año 1970 «tecnología apropiada». Este proyecto fue la primera residencia de contenedores autorizada que se construyó en el condado de San Bernardino.

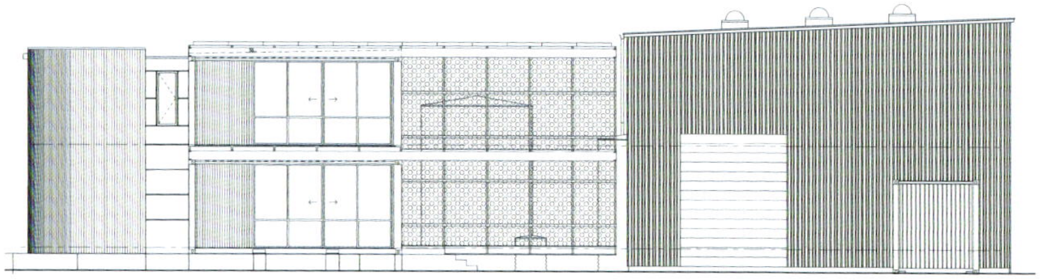

North elevation

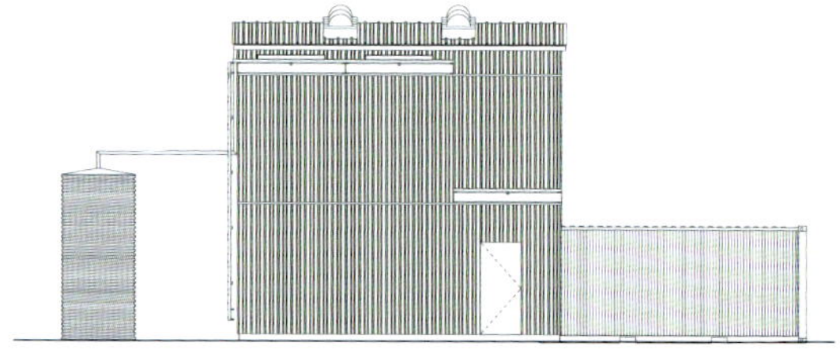

East elevation

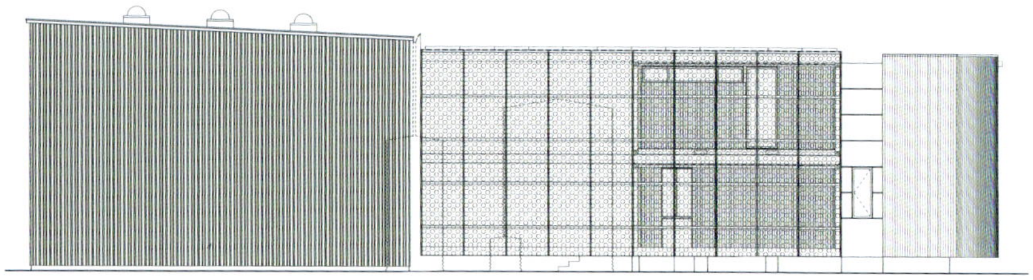

South elevation

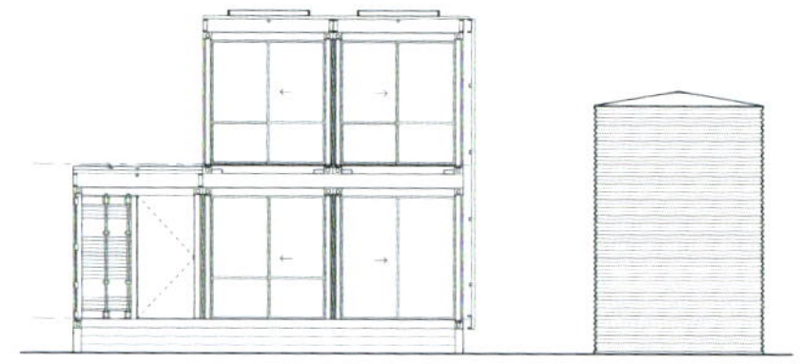

West elevation

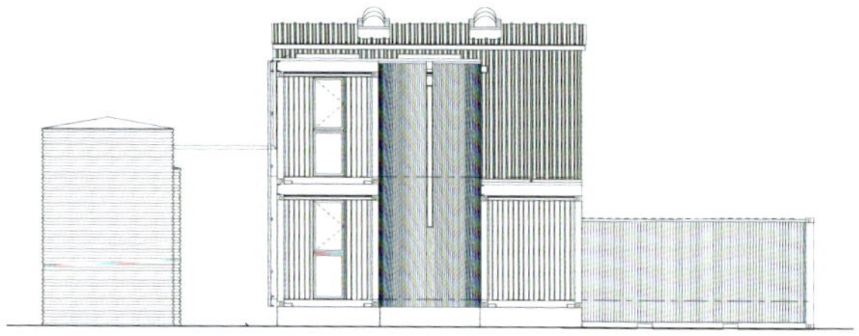

East elevation

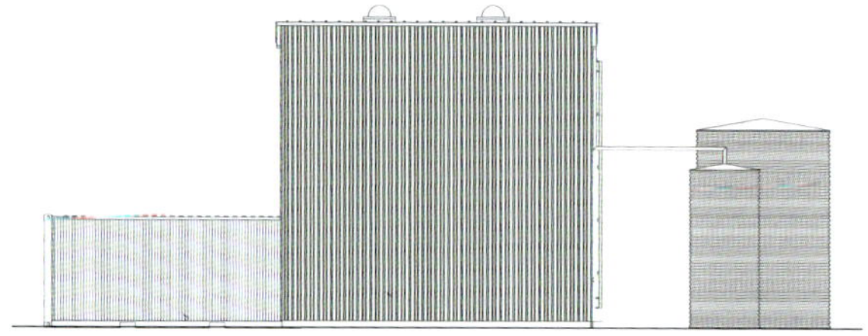

West elevation

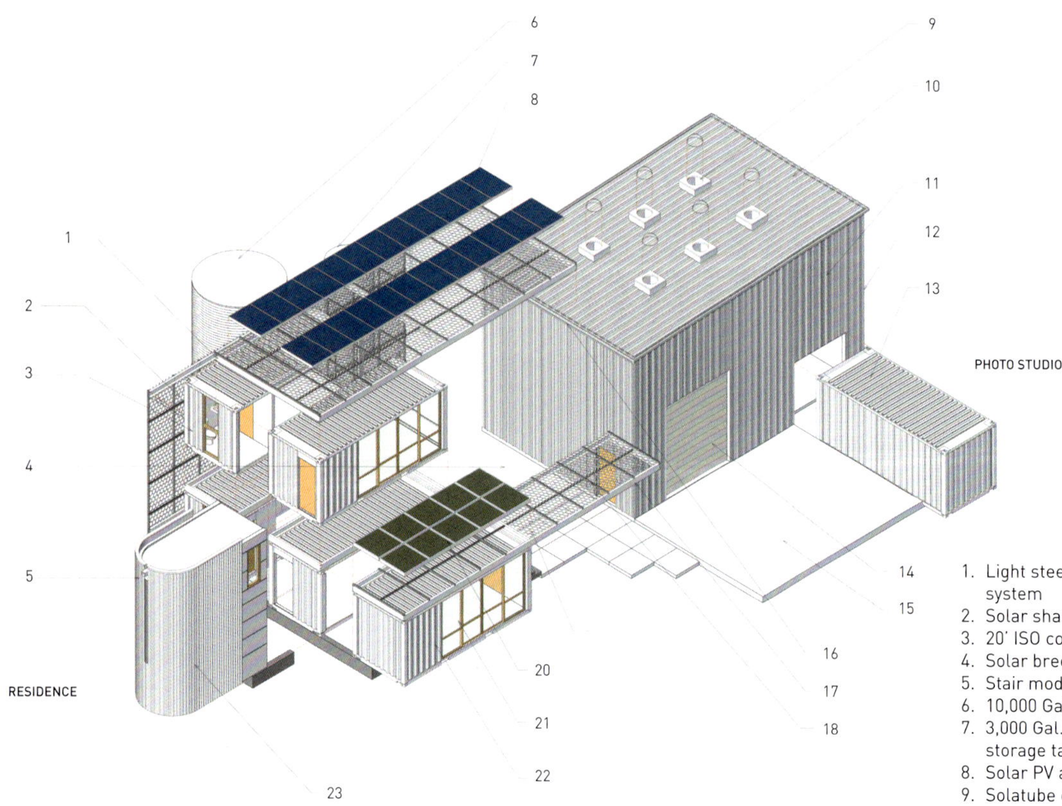

North east exploded axonometric

1. Light steel beam framing system
2. Solar shade canopy
3. 20' ISO containers
4. Solar breezeway
5. Stair module
6. 10,000 Gal. Water storage tank
7. 3,000 Gal. Water harvest storage tank
8. Solar PV array
9. Solatube daylighting
10. Cool roof' steel roof panels
11. Steel wall panels.
12. Butler pre-engineer steel bldg.
13. 0' Iso steel container storage
14. Roll up steel door
15. Parking slab
16. Gutter and water harvesting storage system
17. Lsb framing system
18. Unistrut sub framing system
19. Solar shade canopy
20. Living green roof modules
21. Low 'E'' insulated glazing
22. 20' ISO containers (5)
23. Corrugated matal siding

Perspective view

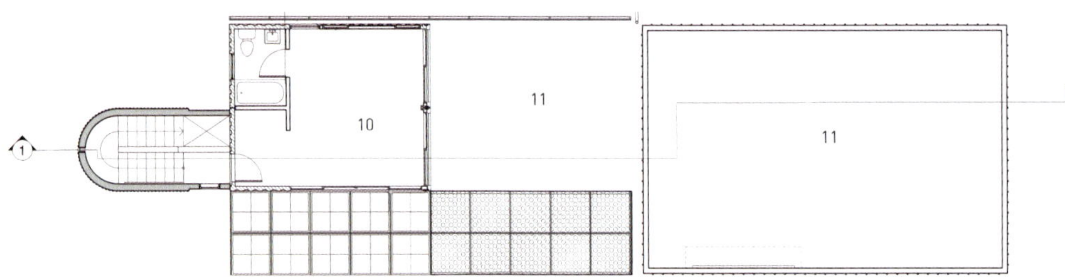

First floor plan

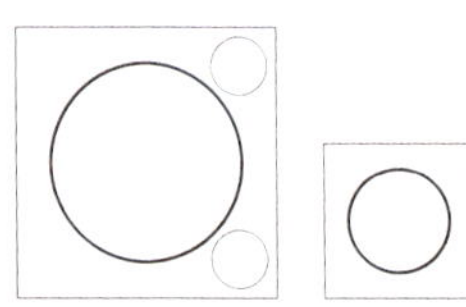

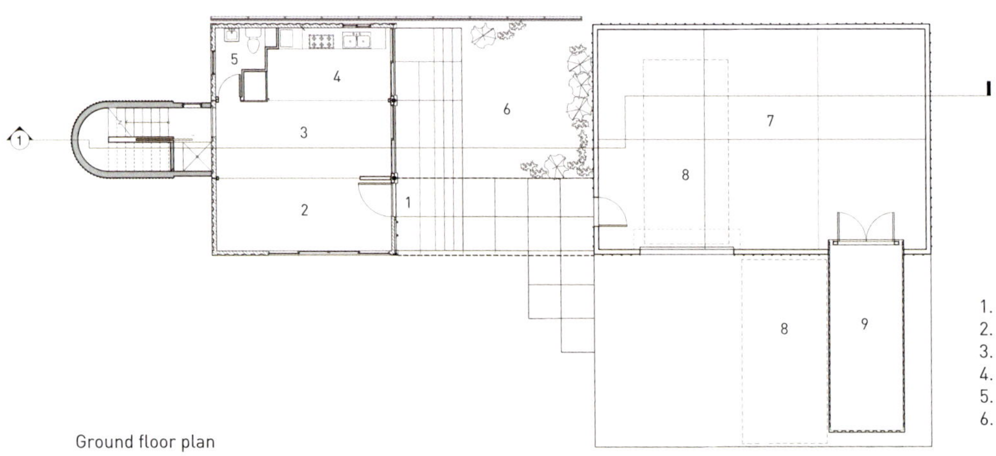

Ground floor plan

1. Entry
2. Living room
3. Dining room
4. Kitchen
5. Bathroom
6. Solar breezeway
7. Photo studio
8. Parking
9. Storage
10. Bedroom
11. Open to bellow

GIANT CONTAINERS

Giant Containers is a global supplier of new, used and modified shipping containers. We offer numerous residential, commercial, retail and industrial projects; whatever the obstacle, an eco-friendly, affordable, custom enclosure is the best solution. Our commitment to quality prefabricated construction and craftsmanship allows us to produce cost-effective sustainable living and working spaces in a timely fashion.

Giant Containers ist ein weltweiter Anbieter von neuen, gebrauchten und modifizierten Containern. Wir bieten zahlreiche Projekte in den Bereichen Wohnen, Gewerbe, Einzelhandel und Industrie an. Egal, um welches Hindernis es sich handelt, eine umweltfreundliche, erschwingliche und maßgefertigte Überdachung ist die beste Lösung. Unser Engagement für hochwertige Fertigbauweise und Handwerkskunst ermöglicht es uns, nachhaltige, kosteneffiziente Wohn- und Arbeitsräume in kürzester Zeit zu realisieren.

Giant Containers est un fournisseur mondial de conteneurs neufs, usagés et modifiés. Nous proposons de nombreux projets résidentiels, commerciaux, de détail et industriels. Quel que soit l'obstacle, une enceinte sur mesure, abordable et respectueuse de l'environnement est la meilleure solution. Notre engagement en faveur d'une construction préfabriquée de qualité et d'un savoir-faire artisanal nous permet de produire des espaces de vie et de travail durables et rentables dans les meilleurs délais.

Giant Containers es un proveedor mundial de contenedores nuevos, usados y modificados. Ofrecemos numerosos proyectos residenciales, comerciales, minoristas e industriales; sea cual sea el obstáculo, un recinto ecológico, asequible y a medida es la mejor solución. Nuestro compromiso con la calidad de la construcción prefabricada y la artesanía nos permite producir espacios de vida y de trabajo sostenibles y rentables en el momento oportuno.

LOUIS VUITTON
Pont Neuf Ideation & Global Logistics Corporation
LV
5
LV MADE

GESU 501100 9
22G0

LOUIS VUITTON MENS TEMPORARY RESIDENCY

Miami, Florida United States | Photos: © Giant Containers

Louis Vuitton approached us with a giant idea for a container installation in Miami to showcase their 2021 spring/summer menswear featuring designs from Virgil Abloh. We've always appreciated their creative approach and knew this would be a project that would allow us to really push the limits of what can be done with containers.

The project consists of 20 HC containers in total, with custom steel structure and openings. Types used are 20' and 40' open side, and 20' double door containers, plus a couple of 20's for signage. Complete with framing, insulation, interior finish, electrical, plus AC on double doors.

Louis Vuitton kontaktierte uns mit einer gigantischen Idee für eine Container-Installation in Miami, um ihre Frühjahr/Sommer 2021 Herrenmode mit Designs von Virgil Abloh zu präsentieren. Wir haben ihre kreative Herangehensweise schon immer geschätzt und wussten, dass dies ein Projekt sein würde, das es uns ermöglichen würde, die Grenzen dessen, was mit Containern gemacht werden kann, wirklich zu erweitern.

Das Projekt besteht aus insgesamt 20 HC-Containern mit Stahlkonstruktion und maßgeschneiderten Öffnungen. Verwendet werden 20'- und 40'-Container mit offener Seite und 20'-Container mit Doppeltür sowie ein Paar 20'-Container für die Beschilderung. Komplett mit Rahmen, Isolierung, Innenausbau, Elektrik und Klimaanlage an Doppeltüren.

Louis Vuitton nous a contactés avec une idée géante d'installation de conteneurs à Miami pour présenter ses vêtements pour hommes printemps/été 2021 avec des dessins de Virgil Abloh. Nous avons toujours apprécié leur approche créative et nous savions que ce projet nous permettrait de repousser les limites de ce qui peut être fait avec des conteneurs.

Le projet consiste en 20 conteneurs HC au total, avec une structure en acier et des ouvertures personnalisées. Les types utilisés sont des conteneurs de 20 et 40 pieds à côtés ouverts, et des conteneurs de 20 pieds à double porte, plus une paire de 20 pieds pour la signalisation. Complet avec cadre, isolation, finition intérieure, électricité et climatisation sur double porte.

Louis Vuitton se puso en contacto con nosotros con una idea gigante para una instalación de contenedores en Miami para mostrar su ropa de hombre primavera/verano 2021 con diseños de Virgil Abloh. Siempre hemos apreciado su enfoque creativo y sabíamos que este sería un proyecto que nos permitiría realmente ampliar los límites de lo que se puede hacer con los contenedores.

El proyecto consta de 20 contenedores HC en total, con estructura de acero y aberturas personalizadas. Los tipos utilizados son 20' y 40' de lado abierto, y contenedores de doble puerta de 20', además de un par de 20's para señalización. Completo con armazón, aislamiento, acabado interior, electricidad y aire acondicionado en las puertas dobles.

LOUIS VUITTON
PANERAI

VUITTON
Pont Neuf Ideation
& Global Logistics
Corporation

MADE

STACKT MARKET

Toronto, Canada | Photos: © Industryous Photography

As one of the largest shipping container market in North America, STACKT is ambitious in both its scale and its plan. On the ground level the new containers thread in and out to create a network of detached buildings with single and double-height interiors. These were retrofitted to provide heating, cooling, as well as the necessary power and water infrastructure to support businesses. Ramps ensure accessibility for strollers and mobility devices. The containers' arrangement creates side streets that enhance the pedestrian experience, and courtyards ideal for cultural programming. While containers conventionally lend themselves to grid-like formations, on the third storey reclaimed containers zigzag across the site, providing some dynamism and presence from Bathurst Street, the condo towers and vantage points on the Gardiner Expressway. The storefronts are deliberately uniform to reduce visual clutter and level the playing field between the independent tenants and their more experienced neighbours, and with some of the units reserved for popups, a visit is like a treasure hunt to discover new vendors with each season.

Stackt, Kanadas größter Markt für Schiffscontainer, ist sowohl vom Umfang als auch vom Plan her ehrgeizig. Im Erdgeschoss werden die neuen Container zu einem Netz von freistehenden Gebäuden mit ein- und zweigeschossigen Innenräumen zusammengefügt. Diese Gebäude wurden so umgerüstet, dass sie Heizung und Kühlung sowie die für kleine Unternehmen erforderliche Strom- und Wasserinfrastruktur bieten. Rampen gewährleisten die Zugänglichkeit für Kinderwagen und Mobilitätshilfen. Durch die Anordnung der Container entstehen Seitenstraßen, die die Fußgängerfreundlichkeit erhöhen, und Innenhöfe, die sich für kulturelle Veranstaltungen eignen. Während sich die Container normalerweise für ein Raster eignen, verlaufen sie im dritten Stock im Zickzack über das Gelände und verleihen der Bathurst Street, den Wohntürmen und der Aussicht auf den Gardiner Expressway Dynamik und Präsenz. Die Schaufenster sind absichtlich einheitlich gestaltet, um die visuelle Unordnung zu reduzieren und das Spielfeld zwischen unabhängigen Mietern und ihren erfahreneren Nachbarn zu ebnen, und da einige der Einheiten für Pop-ups reserviert sind, ist ein Besuch wie eine Schatzsuche, bei der man mit jeder Saison neue Anbieter entdeckt.

Stackt, le plus grand marché de conteneurs d'expédition du Canada, est ambitieux tant par son échelle que par son plan. Au rez-de-chaussée, les nouveaux conteneurs sont reliés entre eux pour créer un réseau de bâtiments autonomes avec des intérieurs à une ou deux hauteurs. Ces bâtiments ont été modernisés pour fournir le chauffage et la climatisation, ainsi que l'infrastructure électrique et d'eau nécessaire aux petites entreprises. Les rampes assurent l'accessibilité aux poussettes et aux appareils de mobilité. La disposition des conteneurs crée des rues latérales qui améliorent l'expérience des piétons et des cours idéales pour les programmes culturels. Alors que les conteneurs se prêtent traditionnellement à des formations en grille, au troisième étage, les conteneurs récupérés zigzaguent sur le site, apportant dynamisme et présence depuis la rue Bathurst, les tours de condominiums et les vues sur l'autoroute Gardiner. Les devantures sont délibérément uniformes afin de réduire l'encombrement visuel et de mettre sur un pied d'égalité les locataires indépendants et leurs voisins plus expérimentés, et comme certaines unités sont réservées aux pop-ups, une visite ressemble à une chasse au trésor pour découvrir de nouveaux vendeurs à chaque saison.

Stackt, el mayor mercado de contenedores marítimos de Canadá, es ambicioso tanto en su escala como en su plan. En la planta baja, los nuevos contenedores se enhebran para crear una red de edificios independientes con interiores de una y dos alturas. Estos edificios se acondicionaron para proporcionar calefacción y refrigeración, así como la infraestructura eléctrica y de agua necesaria para las pequeñas empresas. Las rampas garantizan la accesibilidad para cochecitos y dispositivos de movilidad. La disposición de los contenedores crea calles laterales que mejoran la experiencia peatonal y patios ideales para programas culturales. Mientras que los contenedores se prestan convencionalmente a formaciones cuadriculadas, en la tercera planta los contenedores recuperados zigzaguean por el solar, aportando dinamismo y presencia desde la calle Bathurst, las torres de condominios y los miradores de la autopista Gardiner. Los escaparates son deliberadamente uniformes para reducir el desorden visual e igualar las condiciones entre los inquilinos independientes y sus vecinos más experimentados, y con algunas de las unidades reservadas para pop-ups, una visita es como una búsqueda del tesoro para descubrir nuevos vendedores con cada temporada.

YOU'RE TOTALLY NAILING THIS ADULT THING
500px
Photo by Briony Douglas
イーグル
トーキョー

22GG
GCSU 501100 9
RUNNING LATE?

flow

BREWERY

500px
stackt
Photo by Thomas Fung
500px
stackt
Photo by Jackson Carvalho
STACKT
25GG GCSU 501094 9
SINAI HEALTH
25GG GCSU 501097 5
PUSH
4-103
@MACKHOUSE.INC
25GG GCSU 501095 4
GCSU 501077 0

JOMO
STUDIO

flow

HADVD ARQUITECTOS

Arq. Hugo A. Amparán de León
Arq. Carlos E. Villegas Duarte

HADVD Arquitectos is a firm specialising in architectural design, with a team of professionals who provide a highly qualified service. Passionate about architecture with years of experience, their aim is to take architecture as a pretext to bring dreams, ideas and concepts to life spatially.
HADVD offers a wide range of medium and large scale architectural services, always focusing on the small details that constitute the architectural design process.

HADVD Arquitectos ist ein auf architektonische Entwürfe spezialisiertes Büro mit einem Team von Fachleuten, die einen hochqualifizierten Service bieten. Ihre Leidenschaft für Architektur und ihre jahrelange Erfahrung zielen darauf ab, die Architektur als Vorwand zu nehmen, um Träume, Ideen und Konzepte räumlich zu verwirklichen.
HADVD bietet ein breites Spektrum an mittleren und großen architektonischen Dienstleistungen an, wobei wir uns immer auf die kleinen Details konzentrieren, die den architektonischen Entwurfsprozess ausmachen.

HADVD Arquitectos est un cabinet spécialisé dans la conception architecturale, avec une équipe de professionnels qui fournissent un service hautement qualifié. Passionnés d'architecture et forts de plusieurs années d'expérience, leur objectif est de prendre l'architecture comme prétexte pour donner vie spatialement aux rêves, aux idées et aux concepts.
HADVD propose un large éventail de services d'architecture à moyenne et grande échelle, en se concentrant toujours sur les petits détails qui constituent le processus de conception architecturale.

HADVD Arquitectos es una firma especializada en diseño arquitectónico, que cuenta con un equipo de profesionales que brindan un servicio altamente calificado. Apasionados por la arquitectura con un recorrido de años de experiencia, su objetivo es tomar la arquitectura como un pretexto para aterrizar sueños, ideas y conceptos espacialmente.
HADVD Arquitectos ofrece una amplia línea de servicios arquitectónicos de mediana y alta escala, siempre enfocándose en los pequeños detalles que constituyen el proceso de diseño arquitectónico.

0°
8440

0°

COºRDENADA CENTRO DE DISEÑO

Ciudad Juárez, Chihuahua, México | Photos: © Oscar Hernández

COºRDENADA Design Centre was conceived as a living showroom, a platform for dialogue around design. Located in a region where the architectural project and the culture towards planning is low, a space is developed that encourages a constant dialogue in search of the development of the city, where different disciplines such as architecture, design, engineering and art merge, aiming for a better quality of life accompanied by professionals who nurture the new environment of our cities.
The design of the corporate space contains a line of industrial architecture that stands out in the city, including the reuse of train containers as the building's distribution block that blends with materials such as glass, metal and structural beams visible from inside the building, enhancing its main feature. At the same time, the interior maintains a connection with the environment. Inspired by the golf course it adjoins, a strip of carpeting is created to bring the outdoor environment into the building, a sort of continuation of the green area.
With the contrasting play of colours of the furniture and the characteristics of the systems, the aim is to create a changing, comfortable and innovative space that connects the different types of design and encourages collaboration through its flexible spaces.

Das COºRDENADA Designzentrum wurde als lebendiger Showroom konzipiert, eine Plattform für den Dialog über Design. In einer Region, in der das architektonische Projekt und die Planungskultur gering sind, entsteht ein Raum, der zu einem ständigen Dialog über die Entwicklung der Stadt anregt, in dem verschiedene Disziplinen wie Architektur, Design, Ingenieurwesen und Kunst miteinander verschmelzen, um eine bessere Lebensqualität zu erreichen, begleitet von Fachleuten, die die neue Umgebung unserer Städte pflegen.
Das Design der Geschäftsräume enthält eine Linie industrieller Architektur, die in der Stadt hervorsticht, einschließlich der Wiederverwendung von Zugcontainern als Verteilerblock des Gebäudes, der sich mit Materialien wie Glas, Metall und strukturellen Trägern, die vom Inneren des Gebäudes aus sichtbar sind, vermischt und sein Hauptmerkmal hervorhebt. Gleichzeitig bleibt der Innenraum mit der Umwelt in Verbindung. In Anlehnung an den angrenzenden Golfplatz wurde ein Teppichbodenstreifen angelegt, der den Außenbereich in das Gebäude holt und eine Art Fortsetzung der Grünfläche darstellt.
Mit dem kontrastreichen Farbenspiel der Möbel und den Eigenschaften der Systeme soll ein sich wandelnder, komfortabler und innovativer Raum geschaffen werden, der die verschiedenen Arten von Design miteinander verbindet und durch seine flexiblen Räume die Zusammenarbeit fördert.

Le Centre de Design COºRDENADA a été conçu comme un showroom vivant, une plateforme de dialogue autour du design. Situé dans une région où le projet architectural et la culture de la planification sont faibles, un espace est développé qui encourage un dialogue constant à la recherche du développement de la ville, où différentes disciplines telles que l'architecture, le design, l'ingénierie et l'art fusionnent, visant une meilleure qualité de vie accompagnée par des professionnels qui nourrissent le nouvel environnement de nos villes.
La conception de l'espace d'entreprise contient une ligne d'architecture industrielle qui se distingue dans la ville, notamment la réutilisation de conteneurs de train comme bloc de distribution du bâtiment qui se mêle à des matériaux tels que le verre, le métal et les poutres structurelles visibles de l'intérieur du bâtiment, mettant en valeur sa caractéristique principale. En même temps, l'intérieur maintient un lien avec l'environnement. Inspiré par le terrain de golf qu'il jouxte, une bande de moquette est créée pour faire entrer l'environnement extérieur dans le bâtiment, une sorte de prolongement de l'espace vert.
Avec le jeu de couleurs contrastées du mobilier et les caractéristiques des systèmes, l'objectif est de créer un espace changeant, confortable et innovant qui relie les différents types de conception et encourage la collaboration grâce à ses espaces flexibles.

COºRDENADA Centro de Diseño fue pensado como un Showroom vivo, una plataforma de diálogo en torno al diseño. Ubicado en una región en donde el proyecto arquitectónico y la cultura hacia la planificación es baja, se desarrolla un espacio que fomenta un diálogo constante en búsqueda del desarrollo de la ciudad, en donde se fusionen diferentes disciplinas, como la arquitectura, el diseño, la ingeniería y el arte, teniendo como meta una mejor calidad de vida acompañados de profesionales que nutren el nuevo entorno de nuestras ciudades.
El diseño del espacio corporativo contiene una línea de arquitectura industrial que destaca en la ciudad, incluyendo el re uso de contenedores de tren como bloque distribuidor del edificio que se mezcla con materiales como el vidrio, metal y vigas estructurales visibles desde el interior del edificio, realzando su principal característica. A su vez, el interior mantiene una conexión con el medio ambiente. Inspirado en el campo de golf con el que colinda, se crea una franja con las alfombras que permita llevar el ambiente exterior hacia el interior del edificio, una especie de continuación del área verde.
Con el contrastante juego de colores del mobiliario y las características de los sistemas se busca crear un espacio cambiante, cómodo, e innovador que conecta los diferentes tipos de diseño y que fomenta la colaboración a partir de sus espacios flexibles.

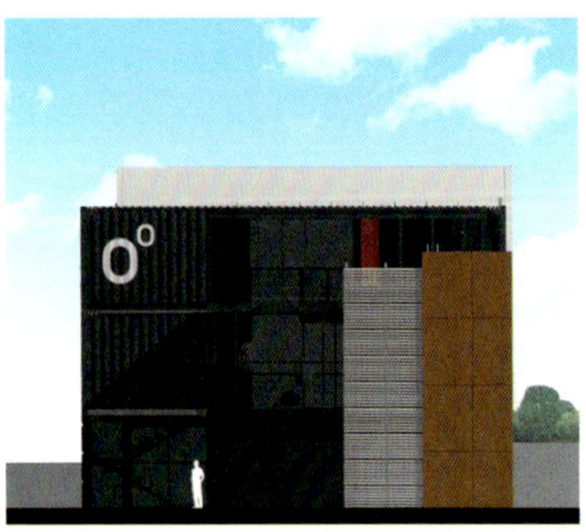

North elevation

West elevation

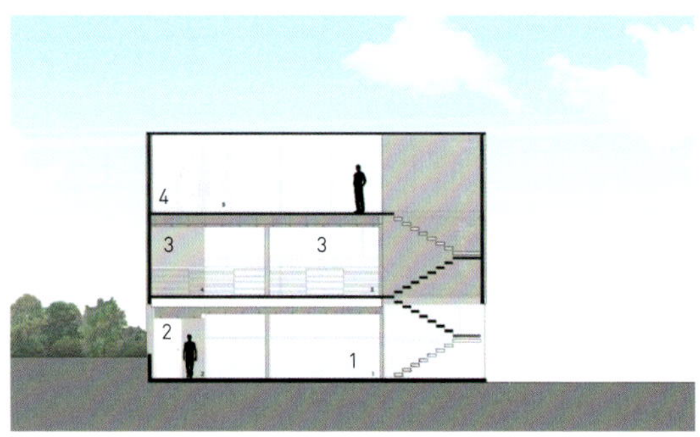

Section 1

1. Show room
2. Bathroom
3. Living room
4. Terrace access

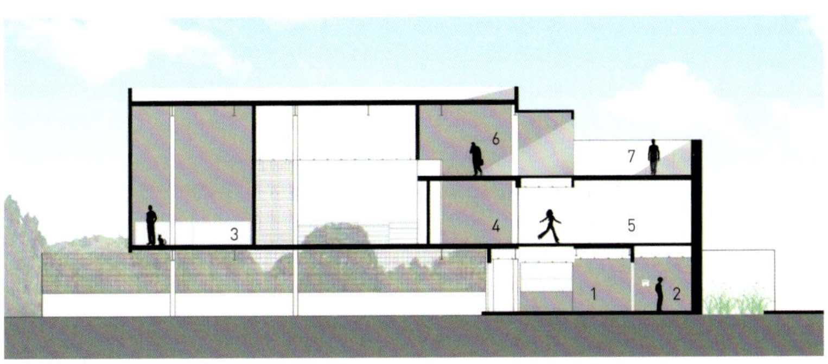

Section 2

1. Show room
2. Bathroom
3. Work area
4. Office
5. Living area
6. Work area
7. Terrace

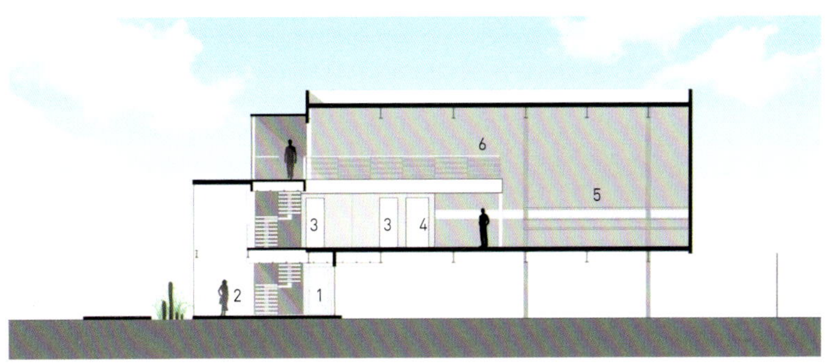

Section 3

1. Show room
2. Living area
3. Bathroom
4. Service
5. Working area
6. Meeting room

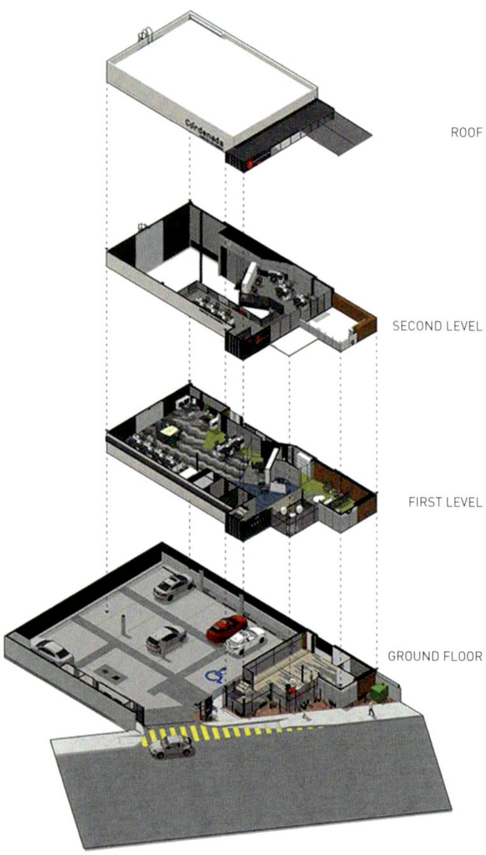

Axonometry

RUTA DE EVACUACION

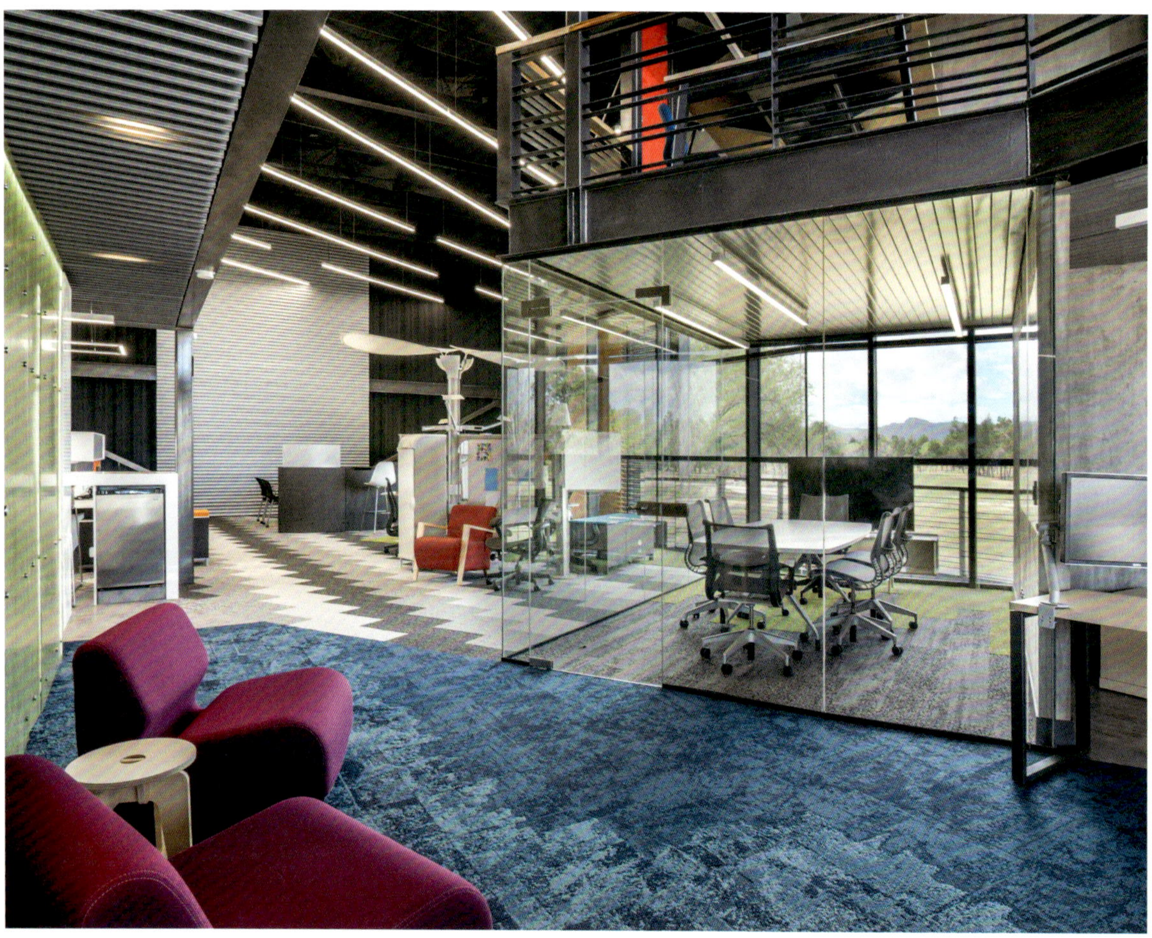

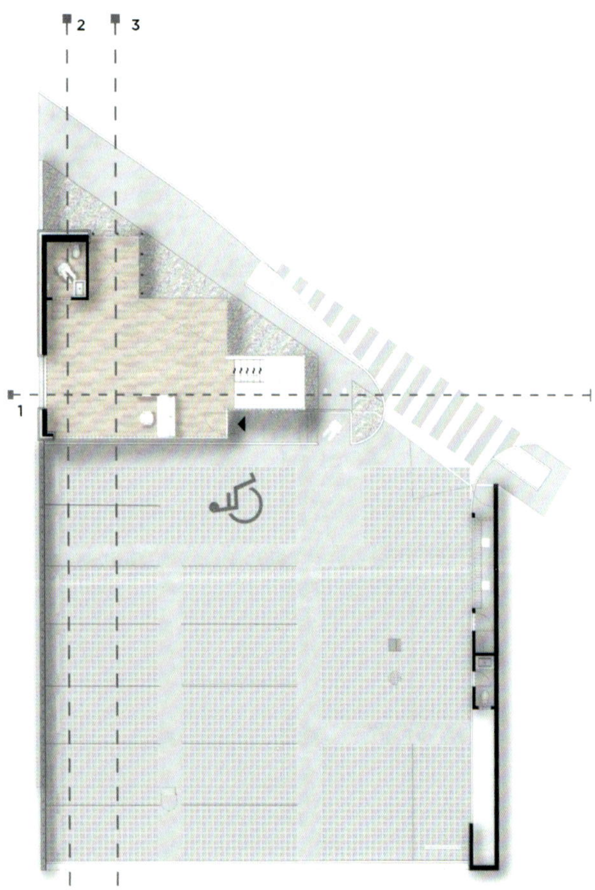

Ground floor plan

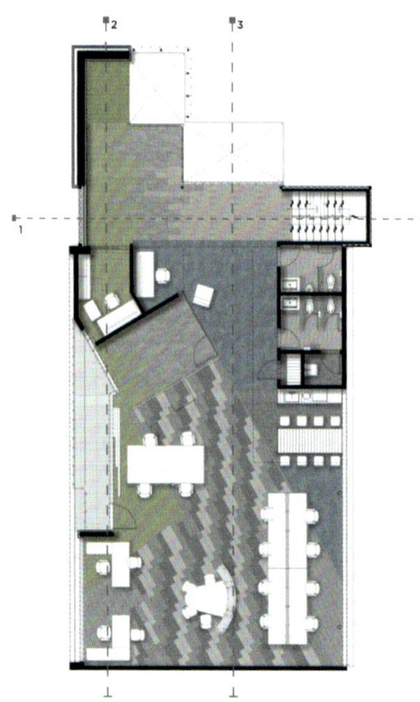

First level plan

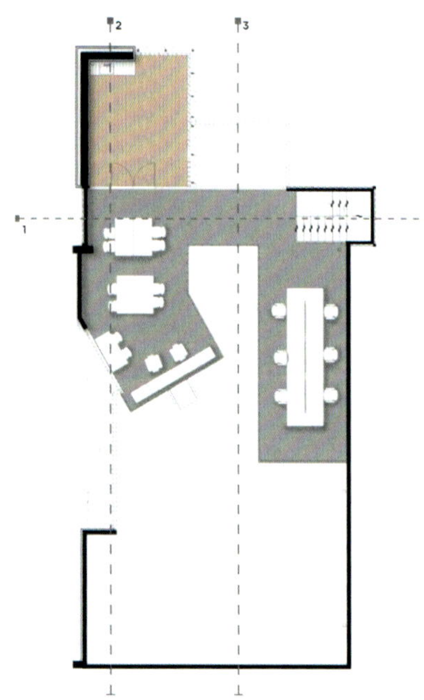

Second level plan

HIGHPOINT TREEHOUSES

Steve Taylor

Steve Taylor of Ladonia, Texas, USA, is a Texas A&M Aggie civil engineer and owner of Highpoint Treehouses. He has a vision, and the "Air Castle" is the flagship treehouse, of a short-term rental destination on the shore of Lake Ralph Hall. He served as the owner, designer, architect, engineer, and contractor on this project. 'Air Castle' is homage to a story from his dad when he was caught daydreaming on the farm as a kid and his father asked, "if he was building air castles". No better way to celebrate the childhood dream than to build an adult treehouse using salvaged materials.

Steve Taylor, aus Ladonia (Texas, USA), ist Bauingenieur an der Texas A&M Aggie und Eigentümer von Highpoint Treehouses. Er hat eine Vision, in der das „Air Castle" das Flaggschiff unter den Baumhäusern ist, ein Kurzzeitvermietungsziel an den Ufern des Lake Ralph Hall. Er war Eigentümer, Designer, Architekt, Ingenieur und Bauunternehmer für dieses Projekt. „Air Castle" ist eine Hommage an eine Anekdote, die ihm sein Vater erzählte, als er als Kind auf dem Bauernhof beim Tagträumen erwischt wurde und sein Vater ihn fragte, „ob er Luftschlösser baue". Es gibt keine bessere Art, Kindheitsträume zu feiern, als ein Baumhaus für Erwachsene aus wiederverwerteten Materialien zu bauen.

Steve Taylor, originaire de Ladonia (Texas, États-Unis), est ingénieur civil à Texas A&M Aggie et propriétaire de Highpoint Treehouses. Il a une vision, où le « Air Castle » est la cabane phare, une destination de location à court terme sur les rives du lac Ralph Hall. Il a été propriétaire, concepteur, architecte, ingénieur et entrepreneur pour ce projet. « Air Castle » est un hommage à une anecdote que son père lui a racontée lorsque, enfant, il a été surpris à rêvasser à la ferme et que son père lui a demandé « s'il construisait des châteaux dans les airs ». Il n'y a pas de meilleure façon de célébrer les rêves d'enfance que de construire une cabane dans un arbre pour adultes à partir de matériaux de récupération.

Steve Taylor, de Ladonia (Texas, EE.UU.), es ingeniero civil de la Texas A&M Aggie y propietario de Highpoint Treehouses. Tiene una visión, donde el «Castillo del Aire» es la casa del árbol insignia, un destino de alquiler a corto plazo a orillas del lago Ralph Hall. Ha sido propietario, diseñador, arquitecto, ingeniero y contratista de este proyecto. «Air Castle» es un homenaje a una anécdota que le contó su padre cuando, de niño, le pilló soñando despierto en la granja y su padre le preguntó «si estaba construyendo castillos en el aire». No hay mejor forma de celebrar el sueño de la infancia que construir una casa en un árbol para adultos con materiales recuperados.

www.highpointtreehouses.com

LADONIA
LAKE RALPH HALL
SMALL TOWN BIG FUTURE
HIGHPOINT TREEHOUSES
ATM
building memories

AIR CASTLE

Ladonia, Texas | Photos: © Joe Shipman - Luminous Productions. Renderings: Element One Studio

Designed for 100 mph winds, the Air Castle, is one of the most unique treehouses using shipping containers. Together with the help from his engineer father, extended family, engineer friends, and network of 30 local expert skilled tradesmen, they developed a layout that capitalized not only the strengths of the containers but framed nature in every room. A purpose-built short-term rental, the design was not driven by a budget, but by creating a unique guest experience to build memories. The goal was to provide a destination that immerses you in nature and as Mr. Taylors' mother says, "allows your soul to catch up". The 6-story and total of 85 step design includes the use of 4 high-cube containers with 2 oriented vertically and 2 others appearing to be cantilevered horizontally 20' off the ground but supported by a bois d arc tree. The vertical containers include the 2-story interior winder stairwell in one and the other has bedrooms / bathroom. The horizontal containers include the living room, kitchen, bathroom, and screened in porch with hot tub. The interior finishes are salvaged from local houses, barns, and on-site black walnut trees.

Das Air Castle, das Windstärken von 160 km/h standhalten kann, ist eines der einzigartigsten Baumhäuser, die aus Schiffscontainern gebaut wurden. Mit Hilfe seines Ingenieursvaters, seiner Familie, befreundeter Ingenieure und eines Netzwerks von 30 lokalen Experten entwickelten sie einen Entwurf, der nicht nur die Vorteile der Container nutzte, sondern auch die Natur in jeden Raum einbezog. Da es sich um eine Kurzzeitvermietung handelt, ging es bei der Gestaltung nicht um das Budget, sondern darum, ein einzigartiges Erlebnis für die Gäste zu schaffen. Ziel war es, ein Reiseziel zu bieten, bei dem man in die Natur eintaucht und, wie die Mutter von Herrn Taylors sagt, „die Seele baumeln lassen kann". Der Entwurf mit insgesamt 6 Stockwerken und 85 Stufen sieht die Verwendung von 4 hohen Würfelcontainern vor, von denen 2 vertikal ausgerichtet sind und 2 horizontal 6 m über dem Boden auskragen, aber von einem Bois d Arc-Baum getragen werden. Zu den vertikalen Containern gehört die zweigeschossige Wendeltreppe im Inneren des einen Containers, der andere enthält Schlaf-/Badezimmer. Zu den horizontalen Containern gehören das Wohnzimmer, die Küche, das Badezimmer und eine überdachte Veranda mit Whirlpool. Die Innenausstattungen stammen von Häusern, Scheunen und Nussbäumen aus der Region.

Conçu pour résister à des vents de 160 km/h, l'Air Castle est l'une des cabanes les plus uniques construites à partir de conteneurs d'expédition. Avec l'aide de son père ingénieur, de sa famille, d'amis ingénieurs et d'un réseau de 30 experts locaux, ils ont mis au point une conception qui non seulement tirait parti des conteneurs, mais encadrait la nature dans chaque pièce. Comme il s'agit d'une location à court terme, la conception n'était pas une question de budget, mais de création d'une expérience unique pour les clients. L'objectif était de proposer une destination qui vous immerge dans la nature et, comme le dit la mère de M. Taylors, « permet à votre âme de se rattraper ». La conception, 6 étages et 85 marches au total, comprend l'utilisation de 4 grands conteneurs cubiques, dont 2 sont orientés verticalement et 2 en porte-à-faux horizontal à 6 mètres du sol, mais soutenus par un arbre en bois d'arc. Les conteneurs verticaux comprennent un escalier intérieur en spirale à deux étages dans l'un d'entre eux et l'autre comporte des chambres à coucher/salle de bain. Les conteneurs horizontaux comprennent le salon, la cuisine, la salle de bains et un porche couvert avec jacuzzi. Les finitions intérieures proviennent de maisons, de granges et de noyers de la région.

Diseñado para soportar vientos de 160 km/h, el Air Castle es una de las casas en el árbol más singulares construidas con contenedores de transporte. Con la ayuda de su padre ingeniero, su familia, amigos ingenieros y una red de 30 expertos locales, desarrollaron un diseño que no sólo aprovechaba las ventajas de los contenedores, sino que enmarcaba la naturaleza en cada habitación. Al tratarse de un alquiler a corto plazo, el diseño no se basó en el presupuesto, sino en la creación de una experiencia única para los huéspedes. El objetivo era ofrecer un destino que te sumerja en la naturaleza y, como dice la madre del Sr. Taylors, «permita que tu alma se ponga al día». El diseño, de 6 plantas y 85 escalones en total, incluye el uso de 4 contenedores de cubo alto, 2 de ellos orientados verticalmente y otros 2 en voladizo horizontal a 6 metros del suelo, pero sostenidos por un árbol de bois d arc. Los contenedores verticales incluyen la escalera de caracol interior de 2 pisos en uno y el otro tiene dormitorios / cuarto de baño. Los contenedores horizontales incluyen el salón, la cocina, el cuarto de baño y un porche cubierto con jacuzzi. Los acabados interiores proceden de casas, graneros y nogales locales.

SMALL TOWN BIG FUTURE
HIGHPOINT TREEHOUSES
ATM
building memories

Roof plan

3D elevation

3D section

"I took a walk
into the woods,
and came out
taller than the trees."
-Henry David Thoreau
KITCHEN

FIRE
DEPT

ANTIQUES
KITCHEN
Farm Fresh
EGGS

cozy

First Aid

BEWARE OF...
WELL... JUST BEWARE
PUMPKINS
HAYRIDES

LADONIA

KG MIMARLIK

Kurtul Erkmen

KG MIMARLIK was founded in 1990. The founder Kurtul Erkmen, graduated from Istanbul State Academy of Fine Arts, also known as Mimar Sinan University, Department of Architecture in 1983 as a master architect. Along with the awards that he got from competitions, he also continues to make a contribution to architecture as a teacher in Istanbul State Academy and a cofounder of AURA-Istanbul. KG MIMARLIK is active in interior design and architecture in Turkey, and has projects in countries such as Turkey, Russia, Romania, Saudi Arabia, Libya, Congo, Kazakhstan, Turkmenistan, Uzbekistan.

www.kgmimarlik.com.tr

KG MIMARLIK wurde im Jahr 1990 gegründet. Ihr Gründer, Kurtul Erkmen, studierte an der Staatlichen Akademie der Schönen Künste in Istanbul, die auch als Mimar Sinan Universität bekannt ist.
Staatliche Akademie der Schönen Künste Istanbul, auch bekannt als Mimar Sinan Universität, Fachbereich Architektur, 1983, als Meisterarchitekt. Neben den Auszeichnungen, die er bei Wettbewerben gewonnen hat, ist er weiterhin als Dozent an der Staatlichen Akademie Istanbul und als Mitbegründer von AURA-Istanbul für die Architektur tätig. KG MIMARLIK ist in der Türkei im Bereich Innenarchitektur und Design tätig und hat Projekte in Ländern wie Russland, Rumänien, Saudi-Arabien, Libyen, Kongo, Kasachstan, Turkmenistan und Usbekistan durchgeführt.

KG MIMARLIK a été fondée en 1990. Son fondateur, Kurtul Erkmen, est diplômé de l'Institut d'études politiques de l'Union européenne. Académie d'État des beaux-arts d'Istanbul, également connue sous le nom d'université Mimar Sinan, département d'architecture, en 1983, en tant que maître architecte. Outre les prix remportés lors de concours, il continue à contribuer à l'architecture en tant que conférencier à l'Académie d'État d'Istanbul et cofondateur d'AURA-Istanbul.
KG MIMARLIK travaille dans le domaine de la décoration intérieure et de l'architecture en Turquie, et a des projets dans des pays comme la Russie, la Roumanie, l'Arabie Saoudite, la Libye, le Congo, le Kazakhstan, le Turkménistan et l'Ouzbékistan.

KG MIMARLIK se fundó en 1990. Su fundador, Kurtul Erkmen, se licenció en la Academia Estatal de Bellas Artes de Estambul, también conocida como Universidad Mimar Sinan, Departamento de Arquitectura, en 1983, como maestro arquitecto. Además de los premios obtenidos en concursos, también sigue contribuyendo a la arquitectura como profesor en la Academia Estatal de Estambul y cofundador de AURA-Estambul.
KG MIMARLIK trabaja en diseño de interiores y arquitectura en Turquía, y tiene proyectos en países como Rusia, Rumanía, Arabia Saudí, Libia, Congo, Kazajstán, Turkmenistán y Uzbekistán.

KUMPORT

Istanbul, Turkey | Photos: © Büşra Yeltekin

The subject is the design of a group of buildings for Kumport Port Services and Logistics Industry Trade Co. while rethinking the port and facilities.
The main visual characteristic of the area's function is a space filled with containers. The visual effect and image created by these containers are highlighted in the headquarters building.
The idea of two ships boarding each other determines the planning principles. Thus two office spaces that are split between two alike masses are connected with bridges on each floor. The sea view from the entrance, which is between two blocks that have been separated from each other with an angle and movement horizontally, is also the main focus of this central area.

Das Thema ist der Entwurf eines Gebäudekomplexes für Kumport Port Services and Logistics Industry Trade Co., der den Hafen und seine Einrichtungen neu konzipiert.
Das wichtigste visuelle Merkmal der Funktion des Bereichs ist ein mit Containern gefüllter Raum. Die visuelle Wirkung und das Bild, das durch diese Container entsteht, wird im Hauptgebäude hervorgehoben.
Die Idee, dass sich zwei Schiffe gegenseitig entern, bestimmt die Planungsgrundsätze. So sind zwei Büroräume, die auf zwei gleiche Massen aufgeteilt sind, auf jeder Etage mit Brücken verbunden. Der Blick auf das Meer vom Eingang aus, der sich zwischen zwei schräg und horizontal voneinander getrennten Blöcken befindet, ist auch der Hauptschwerpunkt dieses zentralen Bereichs.

Le thème est la conception d'un ensemble de bâtiments pour Kumport Port Services and Logistics Industry Trade Co. qui repense le port et ses installations.
La principale caractéristique visuelle de la fonction de la zone est un espace rempli de conteneurs. L'effet visuel et l'image créés par ces conteneurs sont mis en valeur dans le bâtiment du siège.
L'idée que deux navires s'abordent l'un l'autre détermine les principes de planification. Ainsi, deux espaces de bureaux, qui sont répartis entre deux masses égales, sont reliés par des ponts à chaque étage. La vue sur la mer depuis l'entrée, qui se trouve entre deux blocs séparés l'un de l'autre par un angle et un mouvement horizontal, est également le point central de cette zone centrale.

El tema es el diseño de un conjunto de edificios para Kumport Port Services and Logistics Industry Trade Co. replanteando el puerto y sus instalaciones.
La principal característica visual de la función de la zona es un espacio lleno de contenedores. El efecto visual y la imagen creados por estos contenedores se destacan en el edificio de la sede.
La idea de dos barcos abordándose mutuamente determina los principios de planificación. Así, dos espacios de oficinas que se reparten entre dos masas iguales, están conectados con puentes en cada planta. La vista del mar desde la entrada, que se encuentra entre dos bloques separados entre sí con un ángulo y un movimiento horizontal, es también el foco principal de esta zona central.

KUMPORT

TTC

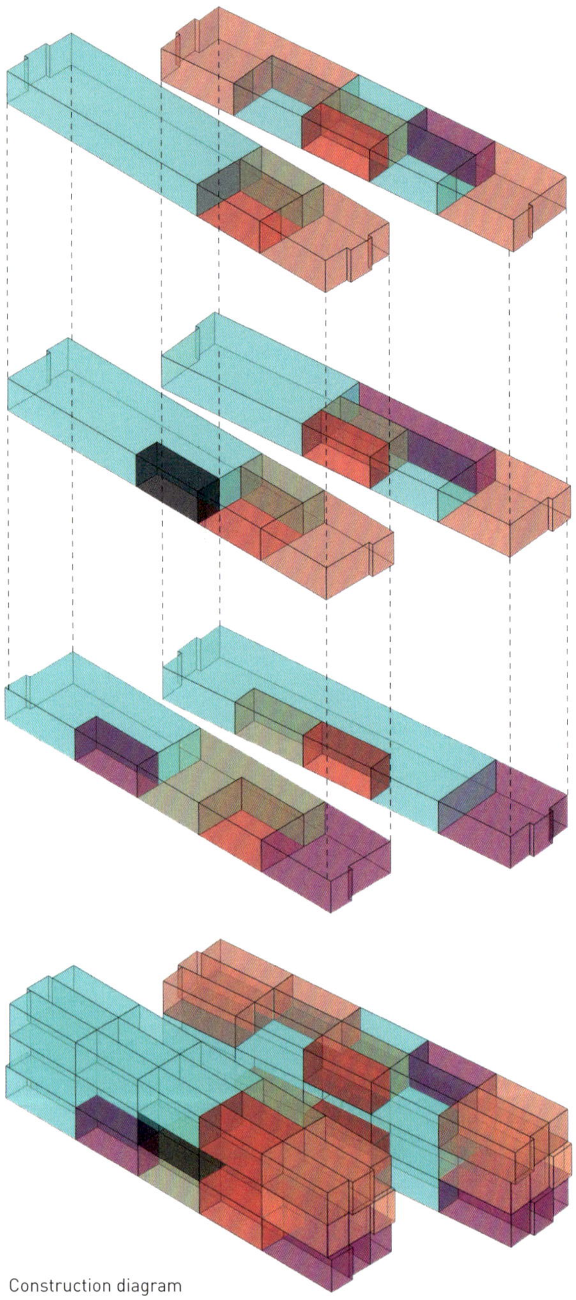
Construction diagram

Core
Management
Circulation
Meeting room
Open office
Technical areas

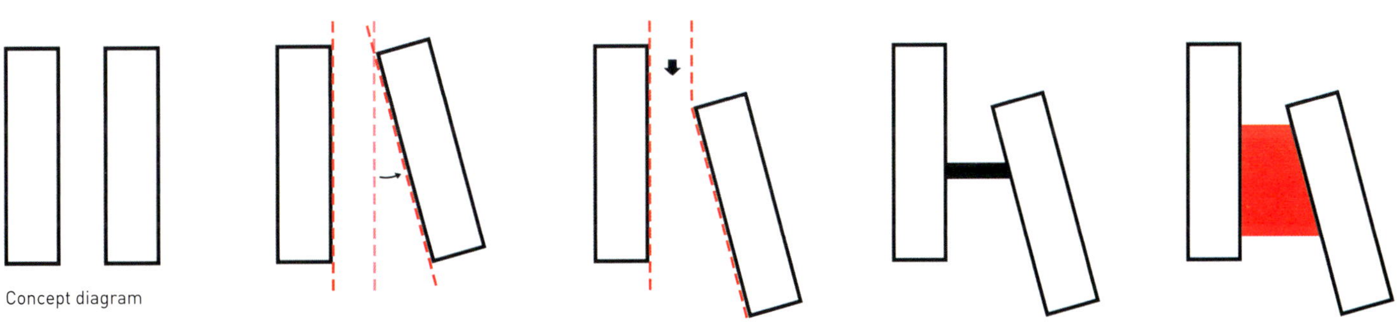

Concept diagram

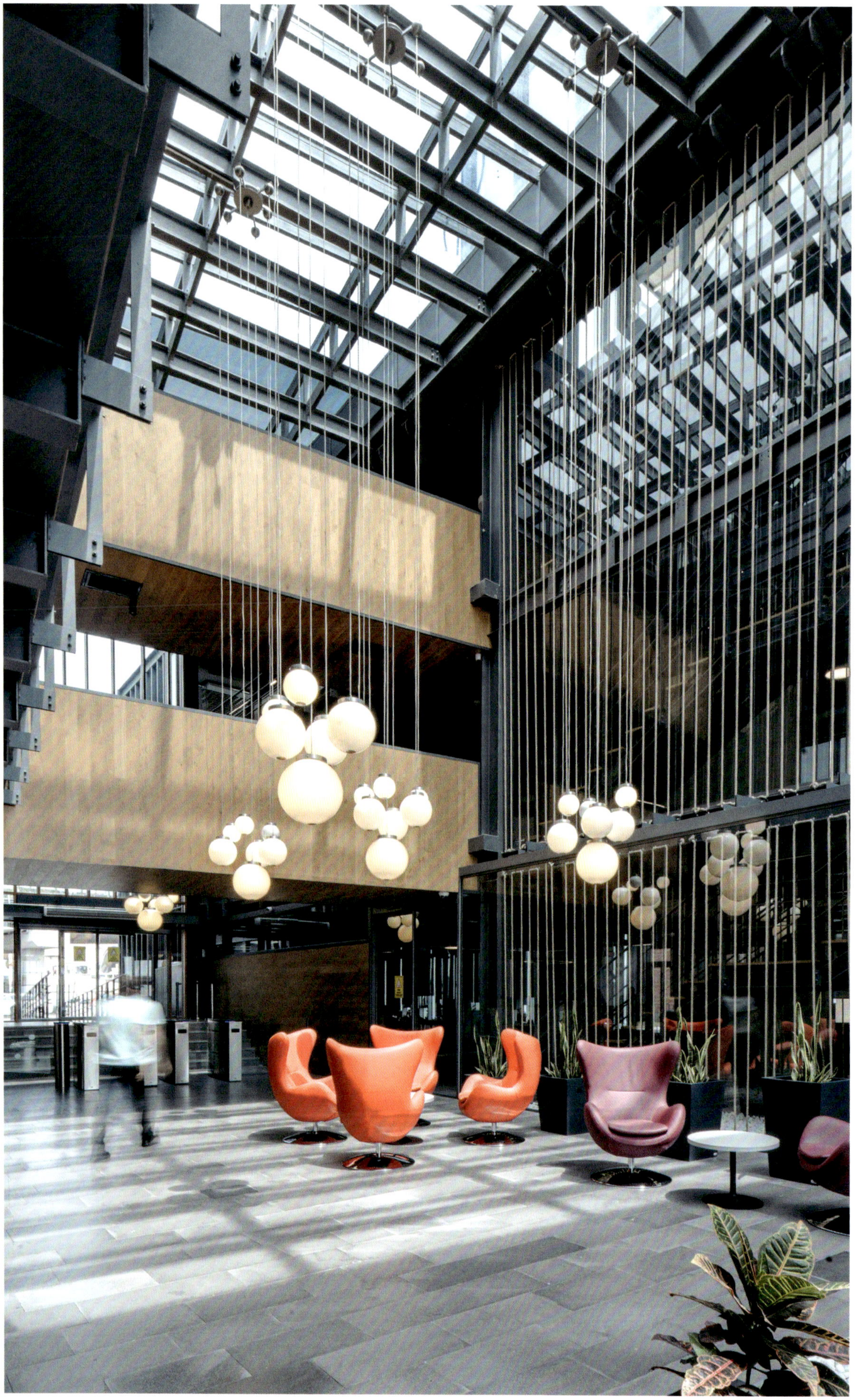

TOPLANTI ODASI
MEETING ROOM

MEIXNER SCHLÜTER WENDT

Florian Schlüter, Claudia Meixner, Martin Wendt

MEIXNER SCHLÜTER WENDT was established in 1997 in Frankfurt/Main by its partners Claudia Meixner, Florian Schlüter and Martin Wendt. The team currently consists of some 50 architects who develop project-specific solutions that take the respective contextual parameters firmly into account.
MEIXNER SCHLÜTER WENDT's designs have received numerous national and international awards and has been the subject of numerous exhibitions, for example, at the Venice Architecture Biennales in 2004, 2006 and 2012.

MEIXNER SCHLÜTER WENDT wurde 1997 in Frankfurt am Main von den Partnern Claudia Meixner, Florian Schlüter und Martin Wendt gegründet. Heute besteht das Team aus rund 50 Architekten, die projektspezifische Lösungen unter sorgfältiger Berücksichtigung der jeweiligen Kontextparameter entwickeln.
Die Entwürfe von MEIXNER SCHLÜTER WENDT wurden mit zahlreichen nationalen und internationalen Preisen ausgezeichnet und waren Gegenstand zahlreicher Ausstellungen, zum Beispiel auf der Architekturbiennale in Venedig 2004, 2006 und 2012.

MEIXNER SCHLÜTER WENDT a été fondé en 1997 à Francfort, en Allemagne, par les associés Claudia Meixner, Florian Schlüter et Martin Wendt. Aujourd'hui, l'équipe se compose d'une cinquantaine d'architectes qui élaborent des solutions spécifiques aux projets en tenant compte des paramètres contextuels respectifs.
Les réalisations de MEIXNER SCHLÜTER WENDT ont reçu de nombreux prix nationaux et internationaux et ont fait l'objet de nombreuses expositions, par exemple à la Biennale d'architecture de Venise en 2004, 2006 et 2012.

MEIXNER SCHLÜTER WENDT fue fundada en 1997 en Frankfurt, Alemania, por sus socios Claudia Meixner, Florian Schlüter y Martin Wendt. En la actualidad, el equipo está formado por unos 50 arquitectos que desarrollan soluciones específicas para cada proyecto teniendo muy en cuenta los respectivos parámetros contextuales.
Los diseños de MEIXNER SCHLÜTER WENDT han recibido numerosos premios nacionales e internacionales y han sido objeto de numerosas exposiciones, por ejemplo, en las Bienales de Arquitectura de Venecia de 2004, 2006 y 2012.

THE DOCKS

Frankfurt am Main, Germany
Photos: © Lars Gruber, Christoph Kraneburg, MEIXNER SCHLÜTER WENDT

Right on the waterfront in Frankfurt's Osthafen district, the new office building, The Docks, comes together with Dock 2.0, a slab-like existing structure, to create a homogenous ensemble. The area surrounding this new office building is dotted with industrial complexes and warehouse facilities and characterized by the uniquely special atmosphere of a container port.
While the façade facing Lindleystrasse is divided up into three sections and boasts a calm appearance, the side giving onto the wet dock has been inspired by bright stacks of shipping containers, with a many-hued façade that integrates the building into the port environment. These features result in the façade structure facing the harbor, which uses prefabricated, folded trapezoidal sheets to form a simple, functional office façade.
The design of the interior spaces with high, inviting foyers along the street frontage greet employees and visitors alike as they enter the building. State-of-the-art office premises with central, excess-width corridors and floor-to-ceiling windows, as well as inviting and lavishly greened sun decks are the most salient features of these offices in their exceptional waterfront location.

Direkt am Wasser im Frankfurter Osthafen verbindet sich das neue Bürogebäude The Docks mit dem Dock 2.0, einem bestehenden Plattenbau, zu einem homogenen Ensemble. Die Umgebung des neuen Bürogebäudes ist geprägt von Industrie- und Lagerkomplexen und der ganz besonderen Atmosphäre eines Containerhafens.
Während die Fassade zur Lindleystraße hin in drei Abschnitte unterteilt ist und ein ruhiges Erscheinungsbild bietet, wurde die dem Nassdock zugewandte Seite von den glänzenden Stapeln der Schiffscontainer inspiriert und integriert das Gebäude mit einer farbenfrohen Fassade in die Hafenumgebung. Aus diesen Merkmalen ergibt sich die Struktur der dem Hafen zugewandten Fassade, die aus vorgefertigten und gefalteten Trapezblechen eine einfache und funktionelle Bürofassade bildet.
Die Gestaltung der Innenräume mit hohen, einladenden Lobbys entlang der Straßenfassade heißt Mitarbeiter und Besucher gleichermaßen willkommen, wenn sie das Gebäude betreten. Hochmoderne Büros mit breiten zentralen Korridoren und raumhohen Fenstern sowie einladende Terrassen mit viel Grün sind die Highlights dieser Büros in außergewöhnlicher Wasserlage.

Situé au bord de l'eau dans le quartier Osthafen de Francfort, le nouvel immeuble de bureaux The Docks rejoint Dock 2.0, une structure de dalles existante, pour créer un ensemble homogène. La zone entourant ce nouvel immeuble de bureaux est parsemée de complexes industriels et d'installations de stockage et se caractérise par l'atmosphère particulière d'un port à conteneurs.
Tandis que la façade donnant sur la Lindleystrasse est divisée en trois parties et présente une apparence calme, le côté donnant sur le bassin à flot a été inspiré par les piles étincelantes de conteneurs d'expédition, avec une façade colorée qui intègre le bâtiment dans l'environnement portuaire. Ces caractéristiques donnent lieu à la structure de la façade donnant sur le port, qui utilise des tôles trapézoïdales préfabriquées et pliées pour former une façade de bureau simple et fonctionnelle.
La conception des espaces intérieurs, avec des halls hauts et accueillants le long de la façade sur rue, accueille les employés et les visiteurs dès leur entrée dans le bâtiment. Des bureaux ultramodernes avec de larges couloirs centraux et des fenêtres allant du sol au plafond, ainsi que des terrasses accueillantes avec une abondante verdure, sont les points forts de ces bureaux dans leur situation exceptionnelle en front de mer.

Justo en el paseo marítimo del distrito Osthafen de Frankfurt, el nuevo edificio de oficinas The Docks se une a Dock 2.0, una estructura existente en forma de losa, para crear un conjunto homogéneo. La zona que rodea este nuevo edificio de oficinas está salpicada de complejos industriales e instalaciones de almacenamiento y se caracteriza por el ambiente singularmente especial de un puerto de contenedores.
Mientras que la fachada que da a la Lindleystrasse está dividida en tres secciones y presenta un aspecto tranquilo, el lado que da al muelle húmedo se ha inspirado en las brillantes pilas de contenedores marítimos, con una fachada de muchos colores que integra el edificio en el entorno portuario. Estas características dan lugar a la estructura de la fachada que da al puerto, que utiliza planchas trapezoidales prefabricadas y plegadas para formar una fachada de oficinas sencilla y funcional.
El diseño de los espacios interiores, con vestíbulos altos y acogedores a lo largo de la fachada a la calle, recibe a empleados y visitantes por igual al entrar en el edificio. Unas oficinas de última generación con pasillos centrales de gran anchura y ventanales que van del suelo al techo, así como unas acogedoras terrazas con abundante vegetación, son las características más destacadas de estas oficinas en su excepcional ubicación frente al mar.

Site plan

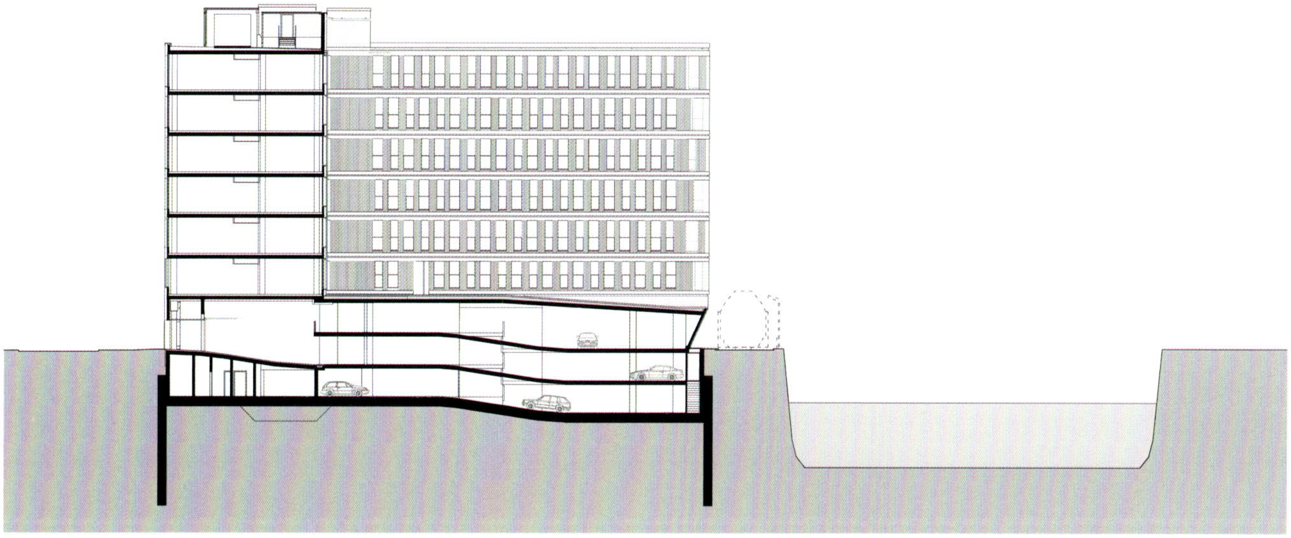

Section

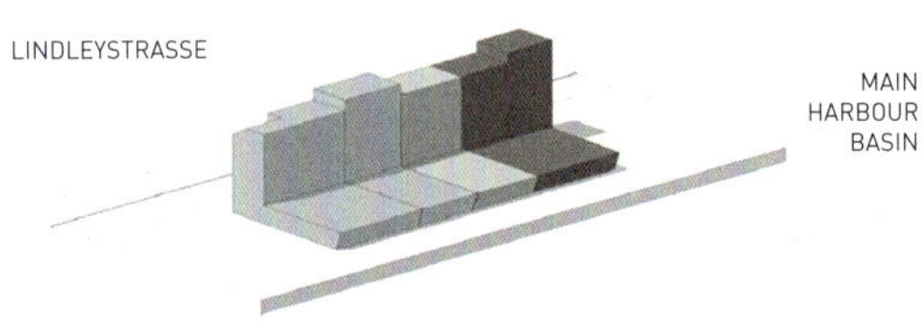

Base body as plinth
and back to the street

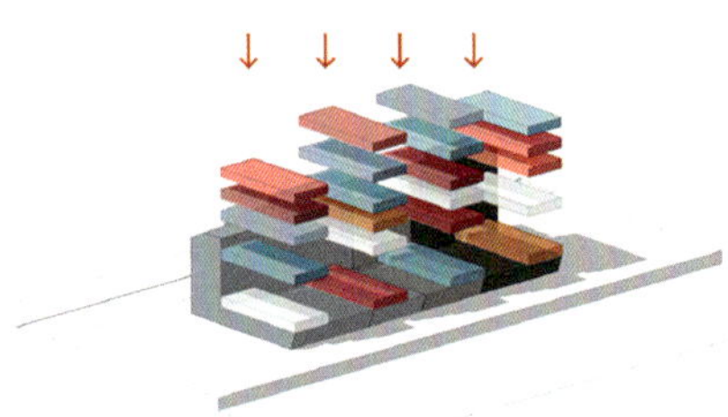

Filling with
container elements

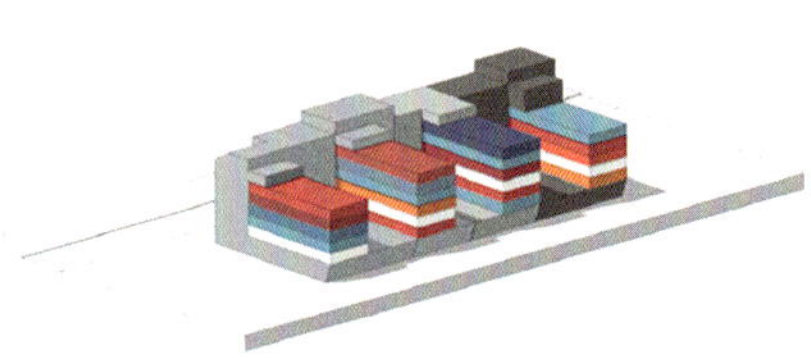

Overall form

Cubature derivation

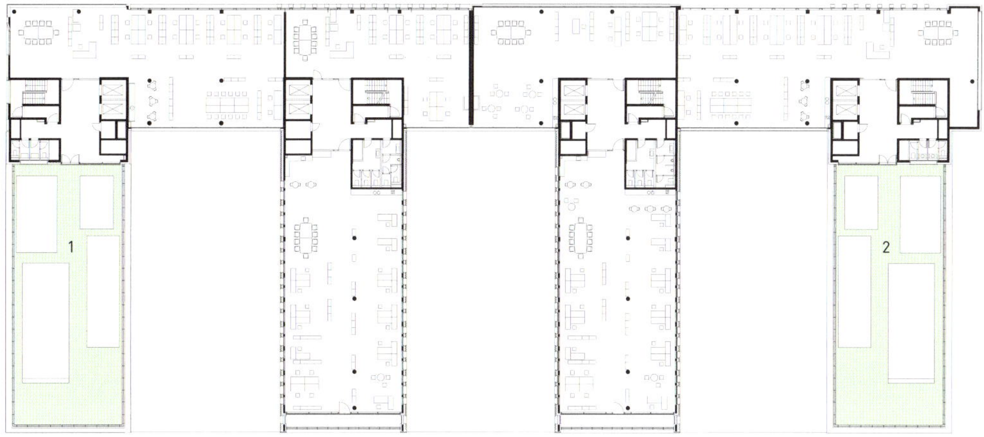

Sixth floor plan

1-2. Green roof terraces
3-4. Logglas

Ground floor plan

1-4. Green inner countyard
4-7. Logglas

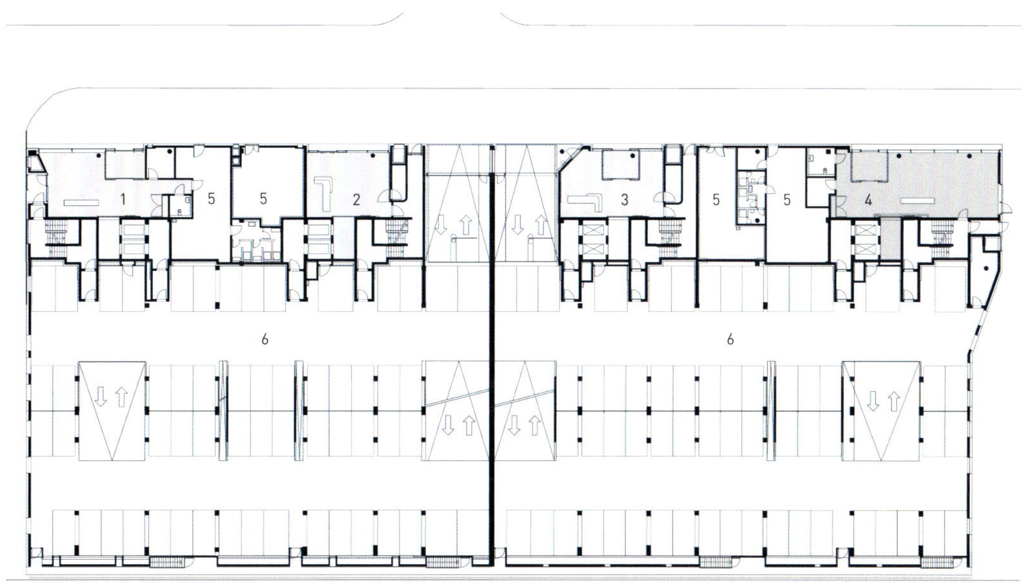

Ground floor plan

1-4. Foyers
5. Side rooms
6. Parking

6
VERLAG FÜR STANDESAMTSWESEN
5
WOLFGANG METZNER VERLAG
4
WOLFGANG METZNER GMBH & CO. KG
3
2
1
SPACES
0
THE LANDING
THE DOCKS LANDING

PAUL MICHAEL DAVIS ARCHITECTS

Paul Michael Davis

Working from a home base in Seattle, Paul Michael Davis and his team design projects at all scales, ranging from art installations to new school buildings. The firm's work is rooted in the values and traditions of the Pacific Northwest, but is also influenced by Paul and his global studies and experiences. PMDA's work has won awards, been widely published, and extends far beyond Seattle. They listen carefully to their clients' needs and the respond to the specific conditions of each site and project differently.

Paul Michael Davis und sein Team mit Sitz in Seattle entwerfen Projekte in allen Größenordnungen, von Kunstinstallationen bis zu neuen Schulgebäuden. Die Arbeit des Unternehmens ist in den Werten und Traditionen des pazifischen Nordwestens verwurzelt, wird aber auch von Paul und seinen weltweiten Studien und Erfahrungen beeinflusst. Die Arbeit der PMDA ist preisgekrönt, wurde vielfach veröffentlicht und reicht weit über Seattle hinaus. Sie haben ein offenes Ohr für die Bedürfnisse ihrer Kunden und gehen auf die spezifischen Bedingungen jedes Standorts und jedes Projekts anders ein.

Basé à Seattle, Paul Michael Davis et son équipe conçoivent des projets à toutes les échelles, des installations artistiques aux nouveaux bâtiments scolaires. Le travail de l'entreprise est ancré dans les valeurs et les traditions du nord-ouest du Pacifique, mais il est également influencé par Paul, ses études et ses expériences internationales. Les travaux du PMDA ont été récompensés, ont fait l'objet de nombreuses publications et dépassent largement le cadre de Seattle. Ils écoutent attentivement les besoins de leurs clients et répondent différemment aux conditions spécifiques de chaque site et projet.

Con sede en Seattle, Paul Michael Davis y su equipo diseñan proyectos a todas las escalas, desde instalaciones artísticas hasta nuevos edificios escolares. El trabajo de la empresa está arraigado en los valores y tradiciones del noroeste del Pacífico, pero también está influido por Paul y sus estudios y experiencias globales. El trabajo de PMDA ha ganado premios, ha sido ampliamente publicado y se extiende mucho más allá de Seattle. Escuchan atentamente las necesidades de sus clientes y responden a las condiciones específicas de cada lugar y proyecto de forma diferente.

www.paulmichaeldavis.com

THE WYSS FAMILY CONTAINER HOUSE

Mercer Island, Washington, United States | Photos: © Mark Woods Photography

As the homeowner, Balthasar Wyss, puts it, "from its earliest days, Seattle was a trade hub." After moving from Switzerland to Seattle, he found the city to be a thriving global center. He was particularly drawn to its port, which is always filled with internationally familiar shipping containers. Rather than respond to the natural environment, as is perhaps the more common way to connect architecture in this region, he wanted to celebrate the place as an important part of a global network. So he decided to hire PMDA with the express request to incorporate shipping containers into their design of an addition to a home for his family of 5. Wyss notes that "each shipping container is unique, its existence carved into its body and visible through scratches and dents as the rust builds patina on the steel boxes." Thus, in this design, the containers are less modular objects to be used as structure, and more found objects celebrated for their uniqueness. A simple architectural volume was added to the existing tract house to "contain" the container. A second container is displayed in the backyard and serves as a multipurpose space for the active family.

Der Besitzer des Hauses, Balthasar Wyss, sagt: „Seattle war von Anfang an ein Einkaufszentrum". Nachdem er aus der Schweiz nach Seattle gezogen war, entdeckte er, dass die Stadt ein blühendes Weltzentrum war. Besonders angetan war er vom Hafen, der immer voller internationaler Schiffscontainer ist. Anstatt auf die natürliche Umgebung zu reagieren, wie es vielleicht die gängigste Art ist, Architektur in dieser Region in Beziehung zu setzen, wollte er das Projekt als wichtigen Teil eines globalen Netzwerks feiern. So beschloss er, die PMDA mit dem ausdrücklichen Wunsch zu beauftragen, Schiffscontainer in seinen Entwurf für eine Hauserweiterung für seine fünfköpfige Familie einzubeziehen. Wyss weist darauf hin, dass „jeder Schiffscontainer ein Unikat ist, dessen Existenz in den Korpus eingraviert und durch Kratzer und Dellen sichtbar ist, während der Rost auf den Stahlboxen Patina bildet". So sind die Container in diesem Entwurf weniger modulare Objekte, die als Struktur dienen, als vielmehr Fundstücke, die für ihre Einzigartigkeit gefeiert werden. Ein einfaches architektonisches Volumen wurde dem bestehenden Haus hinzugefügt, um den Container „einzuschließen". Ein zweiter Container steht im Hinterhof und dient als Mehrzweckraum für die aktive Familie.

Comme le dit son propriétaire, Balthasar Wyss, « dès ses premiers jours, Seattle était un centre commercial ». Après avoir quitté la Suisse pour s'installer à Seattle, il a découvert que la ville était un centre mondial florissant. Il a été particulièrement attiré par son port, toujours rempli de conteneurs de transport international. Au lieu de réagir à l'environnement naturel, comme c'est peut-être la façon la plus courante de relier l'architecture dans cette région, il a voulu célébrer le projet comme une partie importante d'un réseau mondial. Il a donc décidé de faire appel au PMDA en lui demandant expressément d'intégrer des conteneurs maritimes dans son projet d'extension de maison pour sa famille de cinq personnes. Wyss souligne que « chaque conteneur maritime est unique, son existence étant gravée dans son corps et visible à travers les rayures et les bosses, tandis que la rouille crée une patine sur les boîtes en acier ». Ainsi, dans cette conception, les conteneurs sont moins des objets modulaires qui servent de structure, et plus des objets trouvés qui sont célébrés pour leur caractère unique. Un simple volume architectural a été ajouté à la maison existante pour « contenir » le conteneur. Un deuxième conteneur est exposé dans l'arrière-cour et sert d'espace polyvalent pour la famille active.

Como dice el propietario de la casa, Balthasar Wyss,«desde sus primeros días, Seattle fue un centro comercial». Tras mudarse de Suiza a Seattle, descubrió que la ciudad era un próspero centro mundial. Se sintió especialmente atraído por su puerto, siempre lleno de contenedores de transporte internacional. En lugar de responder al entorno natural, como es quizá la forma más habitual de relacionar la arquitectura en esta región, quiso celebrar el proyecto como parte importante de una red mundial. Así que decidió contratar a PMDA con la petición expresa de incorporar contenedores marítimos a su diseño de una ampliación de una casa para su familia de 5 miembros. Wyss señala que «cada contenedor de transporte es único, su existencia tallada en su cuerpo y visible a través de arañazos y abolladuras a medida que el óxido va creando pátina en las cajas de acero». Así, en este diseño, los contenedores son menos objetos modulares que se utilizan como estructura, y más objetos encontrados que se celebran por su singularidad. Se añadió un sencillo volumen arquitectónico a la casa existente para «contener» el contenedor. Un segundo contenedor se exhibe en el patio trasero y sirve como espacio polivalente para la activa familia.

CGIU 222091 9

Second floor plan

Ground floor plan

1. Garage
2. Mud room
3. Family room
4. Kitchen
5. Dining area
6. Outdoor deck
7. Living area
8. Entry
9. Bedroom
10. Laundry room
11. Rec room
12. Terrace
13. Shed (built with shipping containers)
14. Garage below
15. Family room below
16. Closet
17. Shipping container below

UNDER ARMOUR

CGIU 222027 2
22G1
CGIU 222027 2
22G1
MAX. GROSS 30,480 KGS. 67,200 LBS.
TARE 2,010 KGS. 4,430 LBS.
NET 28,470 KGS. 62,770 LBS.
CU. CAP. 33.2 CU.M. 1,170 CU.FT.

TARE
2,010 KGS.
4,430 LBS.
NET
28,470 KGS.
62,770 LBS.
CU.
33.2
1,170

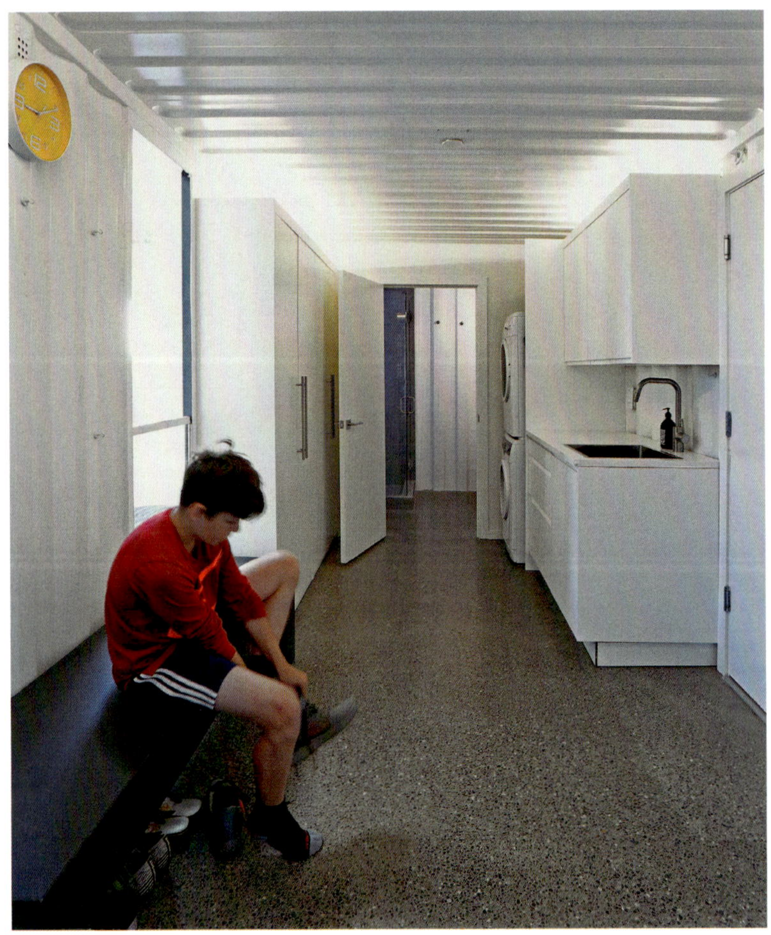

CGIU 222027 2
22G1
87
MAX. GROSS
TARE
NET
CU. CAP.

RINTALA EGGERTSSON ARCHITECTS

Dagur Eggertsson, Sami Rintala
Vibeke Jenssen

Dagur Eggertsson and Sami Rintala are the founders of Rintala Eggertsson Architects, a Norway based architecture firm, which bases its activities around public art, architecture and urban planning. In 2008 Eggertsson and Rintala were joined by Vibeke Jenssen, who is now a full partner in the company. All three studied under Juhani Pallasmaa in Helsinki and are informed by his phenomenological and cross-disciplinary thinking.

Dagur Eggertsson und Sami Rintala sind die Gründer von Rintala Eggertsson Architects, einem norwegischen Architekturbüro mit Schwerpunkt auf öffentlicher Kunst, Architektur und Stadtplanung. Im Jahr 2008 stieß Vibeke Jenssen zu Eggertsson und Rintala, die jetzt vollwertige Partnerin der Kanzlei ist. Alle drei haben bei Juhani Pallasmaa in Helsinki studiert und sind von seinem phänomenologischen und interdisziplinären Denken inspiriert.

Dagur Eggertsson et Sami Rintala sont les fondateurs de Rintala Eggertsson Architects, un cabinet d'architectes basé en Norvège et spécialisé dans l'art public, l'architecture et la planification urbaine. En 2008, Vibeke Jenssen, qui est aujourd'hui associée à part entière du cabinet, a rejoint Eggertsson et Rintala. Tous trois ont étudié avec Juhani Pallasmaa à Helsinki et s'inspirent de sa pensée phénoménologique et interdisciplinaire.

Dagur Eggertsson y Sami Rintala son los fundadores de Rintala Eggertsson Architects, un estudio de arquitectura con sede en Noruega que basa sus actividades en el arte público, la arquitectura y la planificación urbana. En 2008, a Eggertsson y Rintala se les unió Vibeke Jenssen, que ahora es socia de pleno derecho de la empresa. Los tres estudiaron con Juhani Pallasmaa en Helsinki y se inspiran en su pensamiento fenomenológico e interdisciplinar.

FLYT. BATHING INSTALLATIONS FOR FLEISCHER PARK

Moss, Norway | Photos: © Dag Jenssen, Nicholas Ryan Coates

The project is the outcome of an art-in-public-space competition that the municipality of Moss organized in 2018 to revitalize a former industrial area west of the city centre as a part of their 300 year anniversary. The competition was won by Rintala Eggertsson Architects with the proposal FLYT - with several bathing installations placed on floating piers in the sound of Moss. After negotiations with landowners, the project was moved to a nearby location where two of the installations were redesigned to fit with pre-existing piers. A third installation was placed inside the adjacent park to house secondary functions, to strengthen the axis towards the city centre, and to give the park area a more human scale. The third pavilion is set to be realized before the summer of 2021.

The bathing installations consist of two strucures: the diving tower with a lookout platform and a light installation, and the sauna both of which will be open to the public year-round. The installations have drawn inspiration from industrial structures in the area: cranes, chimneys, silos, gantries, etc that have defined the cultural landscape around Moss harbour for more than two centuries.

Das Projekt ist das Ergebnis eines Wettbewerbs für Kunst im öffentlichen Raum, den die Gemeinde Moss 2018 im Rahmen ihres 300-jährigen Jubiläums zur Wiederbelebung eines ehemaligen Industriegebiets westlich des Stadtzentrums ausgeschrieben hatte. Der Wettbewerb wurde von Rintala Eggertsson Architects mit dem Vorschlag FLYT gewonnen, bei dem mehrere Badeeinrichtungen auf Schwimmdocks im Moss-Sund platziert werden. Nach Verhandlungen mit den Grundstückseigentümern wurde das Projekt an einen nahe gelegenen Standort verlegt, wo zwei der Anlagen so umgestaltet wurden, dass sie in die bereits vorhandenen Docks passen. Eine dritte Einrichtung wurde im angrenzenden Park untergebracht, um sekundäre Funktionen unterzubringen, die Achse zum Stadtzentrum zu stärken und dem Parkbereich einen menschlicheren Maßstab zu verleihen. Die Fertigstellung des dritten Pavillons ist für den Sommer 2021 geplant.

Die Badeanlage besteht aus zwei Bauwerken: dem Sprungturm mit Aussichtsplattform und Lichtinstallation und der Sauna, die ganzjährig für die Öffentlichkeit zugänglich sein wird. Die Einrichtungen wurden von den industriellen Strukturen der Region inspiriert: Kräne, Schornsteine, Silos, Schilderbrücken usw., die die Kulturlandschaft um den Hafen von Moss seit mehr als zwei Jahrhunderten prägen.

Le projet est le résultat d'un concours d'art dans l'espace public que la municipalité de Moss a organisé en 2018 pour revitaliser une ancienne zone industrielle à l'ouest du centre-ville dans le cadre de son 300e anniversaire. Le concours a été remporté par Rintala Eggertsson Architects avec la proposition FLYT - avec plusieurs installations de baignade placées sur des quais flottants dans le détroit de Moss. Après des négociations avec les propriétaires fonciers, le projet a été déplacé sur un site voisin où deux des installations ont été redessinées pour s'intégrer aux quais préexistants. Une troisième installation a été placée à l'intérieur du parc adjacent afin d'accueillir des fonctions secondaires, de renforcer l'axe vers le centre-ville et de donner à la zone du parc une échelle plus humaine. L'achèvement du troisième pavillon est prévu pour l'été 2021.

Les installations de baignade se composent de deux structures : le plongeoir avec une plate-forme d'observation et une installation lumineuse, et le sauna, qui sera ouvert au public toute l'année. Les installations ont été inspirées par les structures industrielles de la région : grues, cheminées, silos, portiques, etc. qui définissent le paysage culturel autour du port de Moss depuis plus de deux siècles.

El proyecto es el resultado de un concurso de arte en el espacio público que el municipio de Moss organizó en 2018 para revitalizar una antigua zona industrial al oeste del centro de la ciudad como parte de su 300 aniversario. El concurso lo ganó Rintala Eggertsson Architects con la propuesta FLYT - con varias instalaciones de baño colocadas en muelles flotantes en el sonido de Moss. Tras negociar con los propietarios de los terrenos, el proyecto se trasladó a un lugar cercano donde se rediseñaron dos de las instalaciones para que encajaran en los muelles preexistentes. Una tercera instalación se colocó en el interior del parque adyacente para albergar funciones secundarias, reforzar el eje hacia el centro de la ciudad y dar a la zona del parque una escala más humana. El tercer pabellón está previsto que se realice antes del verano de 2021.

Las instalaciones de baño constan de dos estructuras: la torre de buceo con una plataforma de observación y una instalación de luz, y la sauna, que estarán abiertas al público todo el año. Las instalaciones se han inspirado en las estructuras industriales de la zona: grúas, chimeneas, silos, pórticos, etc. que han definido el paisaje cultural en torno al puerto de Moss durante más de dos siglos.

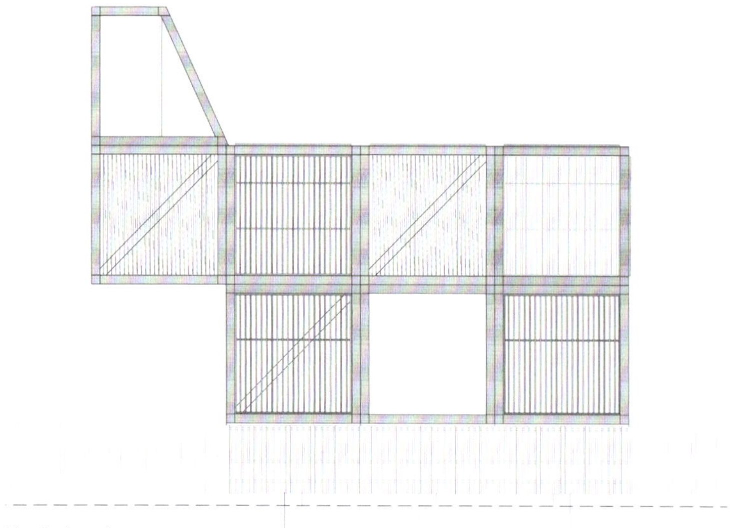

North elevation

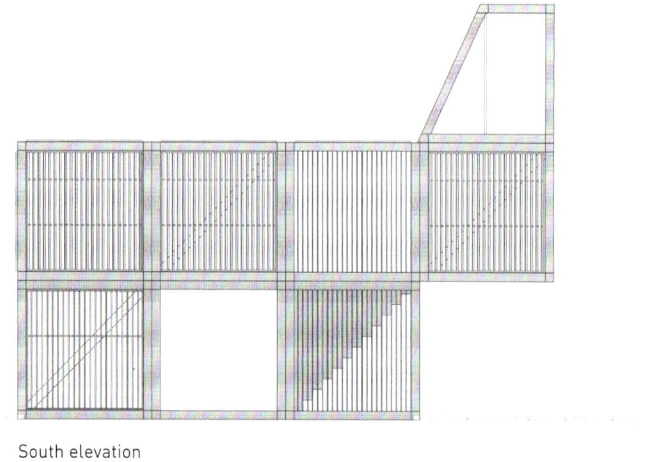

South elevation

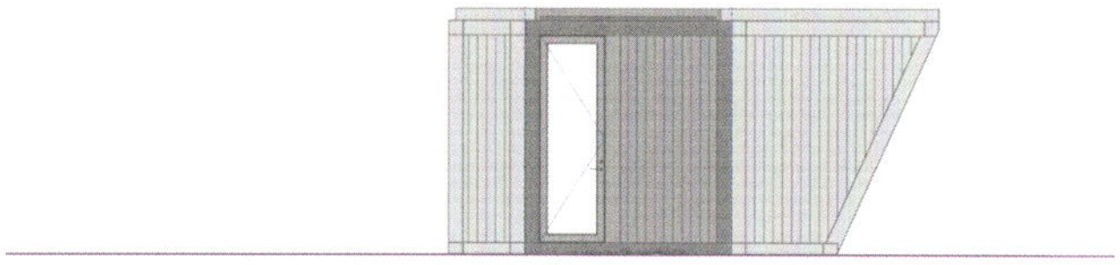

South elevation

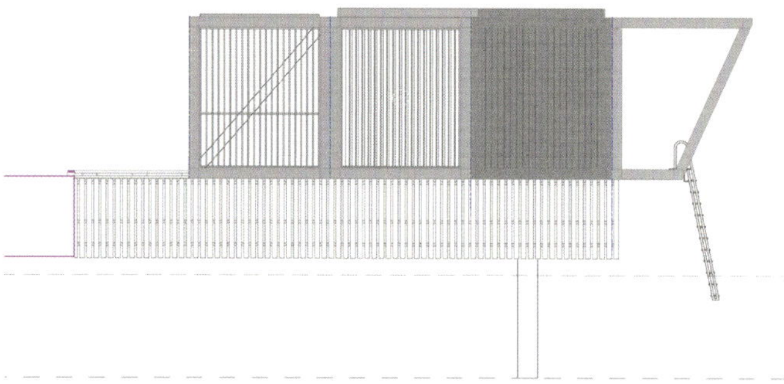

East elevation

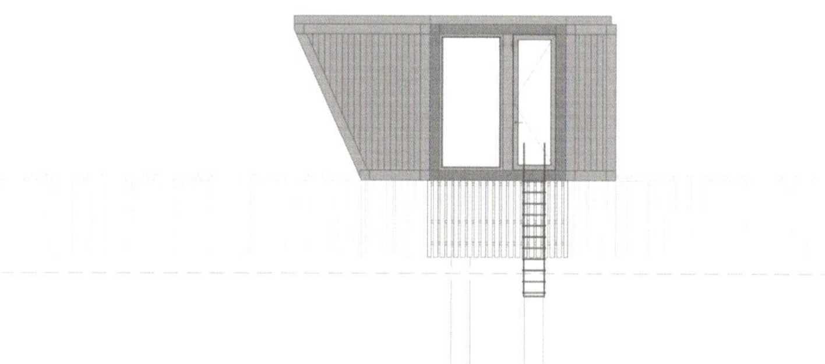

North elevation

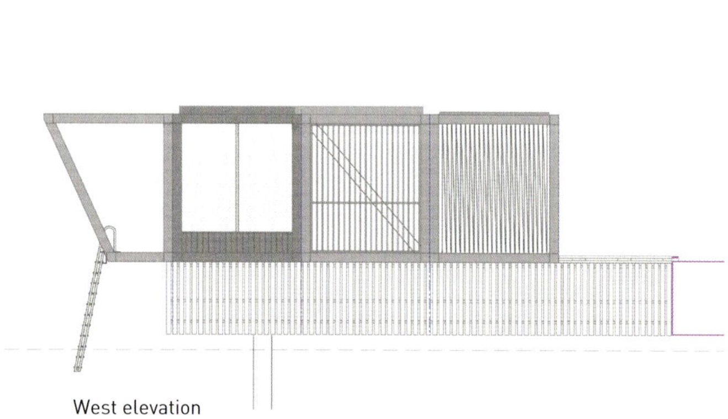

West elevation

DRAGONFLY TREEHOTEL

Harads, Sweden | Photos: © Ryan Koopmans, Peter Lundström

Our proposal for the new Treehotel room was a long horizontal animal-like structure that spans supported between a group of 4-6 pines. The project is placed on a top of the hillside, on the edge of a thicker forest.
The main windows open towards the south and to the wider landscape while the back wall towards north is more sheltering.
In the middle of the interior are common functions: kitchen, dining area and fire place from where one can enter the bedrooms and toilets, spaces which are cantilevered to the main volume.
Facade is made of narrow grey weathered boards. Åspen is a great material here, thanks to its good resistance in northern climate. It is also soft to touch which is important as the same material is exposed to the interior as well. Fixed furniture like beds, kitchen bench and table plus benches is made of oiled thermo treated wood, as are ceiling and floors too.
The idea was to create a small space that is connected to the tree crowns and the landscape outside and that reacts to the different sunlight situations during the day. The horizontal line of the building is supposed to create a harmonious whole with the vertical pine forest.

Unser Vorschlag für das neue Treehotel-Zimmer war eine lange, horizontale, tierförmige Struktur, die sich zwischen einer Gruppe von 4-6 Kiefern erstreckt. Das Projekt liegt hoch am Hang, am Rande eines dichten Waldes.
Die Hauptfenster öffnen sich nach Süden und in die weite Landschaft, während die Rückwand im Norden geschützter ist.
Im Zentrum des Innenraums befinden sich die gemeinsamen Funktionen: die Küche, das Esszimmer und der Kamin, von dem aus man zu den Schlafzimmern und Toiletten gelangt, Räume, die zum Hauptvolumen hin auskragen.
Die Fassade besteht aus schmalen, verwitterten grauen Brettern. Åspen ist in diesem Fall ein hervorragendes Material, da es dem nördlichen Klima gut standhält. Außerdem fühlt es sich weich an, was wichtig ist, da das gleiche Material auch im Innenraum verwendet wird. Die festen Möbel wie die Betten, die Bank und der Küchentisch sowie die Bänke sind aus geöltem, wärmebehandeltem Holz, ebenso wie die Decke und der Boden.
Die Idee war, einen kleinen Raum zu schaffen, der mit den Baumkronen und der Landschaft draußen verbunden ist und auf die verschiedenen Sonnenlichtsituationen während des Tages reagiert. Die horizontale Linie des Gebäudes soll ein harmonisches Ensemble mit dem vertikalen Kiefernwald bilden.

Notre proposition pour la nouvelle chambre du Treehotel était une longue structure horizontale en forme d'animal qui s'étend entre un groupe de 4 à 6 pins. Le projet est situé en haut de la colline, à la lisière d'une forêt plus dense.
Les fenêtres principales s'ouvrent sur le sud et le grand paysage, tandis que le mur arrière au nord est plus abrité.
Au centre de l'intérieur se trouvent les fonctions communes : la cuisine, la salle à manger et la cheminée, à partir desquelles on accède aux chambres et aux toilettes, des espaces en porte-à-faux vers le volume principal.
La façade est constituée de planches grises étroites et usées par le temps. L'Åspen est un matériau idéal dans ce cas, grâce à sa bonne résistance au climat nordique. Il est également doux au toucher, ce qui est important, car le même matériau est exposé à l'intérieur également. Les meubles fixes, tels que les lits, le banc et la table de cuisine, ainsi que les bancs, sont en bois huilé et traité thermiquement, tout comme le plafond et le sol.
L'idée était de créer un petit espace relié à la cime des arbres et au paysage extérieur et réagissant aux différentes situations d'ensoleillement de la journée. La ligne horizontale du bâtiment doit créer un ensemble harmonieux avec la pinède verticale.

Nuestra propuesta para la nueva habitación del Treehotel fue una larga estructura horizontal en forma de animal que se extiende apoyada entre un grupo de 4-6 pinos. El proyecto se sitúa en lo alto de la ladera, en el límite de un bosque más espeso.
Las ventanas principales se abren hacia el sur y al paisaje más amplio, mientras que la pared trasera hacia el norte es más abrigada.
En el centro del interior se encuentran las funciones comunes: la cocina, el comedor y la chimenea, desde donde se accede a los dormitorios y los aseos, espacios que están en voladizo hacia el volumen principal.
La fachada está hecha de estrechas tablas grises desgastadas. El Åspen es un gran material en este caso, gracias a su buena resistencia en el clima del norte. También es suave al tacto, lo que es importante, ya que el mismo material está expuesto en el interior también. Los muebles fijos, como las camas, el banco y la mesa de la cocina, además de los bancos, son de madera tratada térmicamente con aceite, al igual que el techo y el suelo.
La idea era crear un pequeño espacio que estuviera conectado con las copas de los árboles y el paisaje exterior y que reaccionara a las diferentes situaciones de luz solar durante el día. La línea horizontal del edificio debe crear un conjunto armonioso con el pinar vertical.

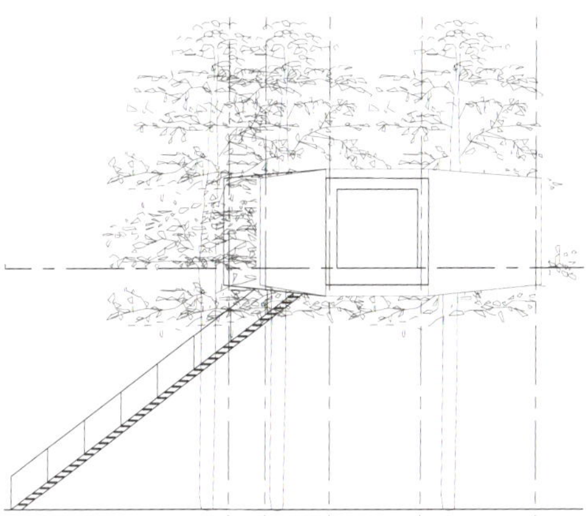

Elevation

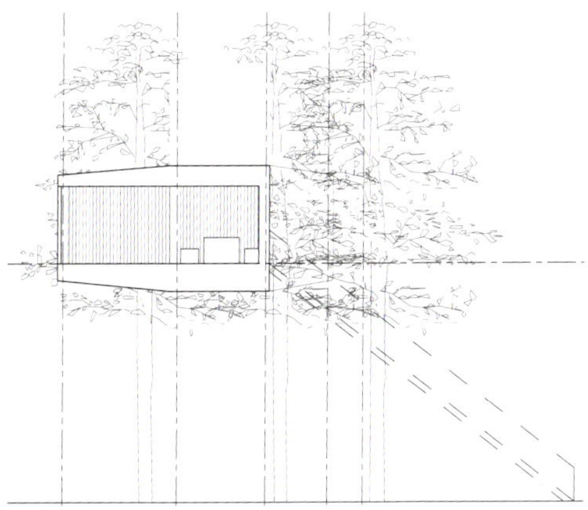

Section

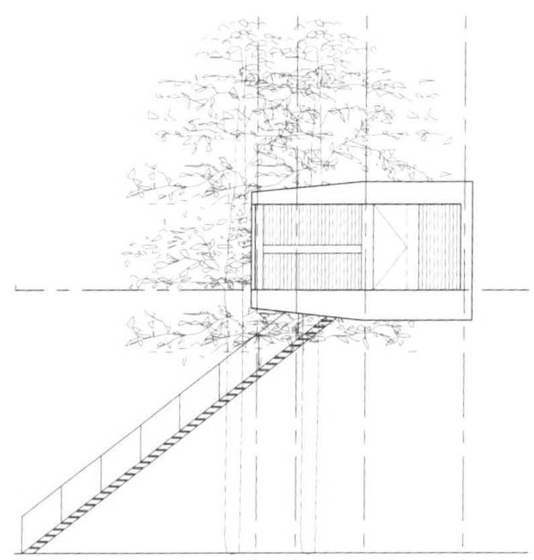

Section

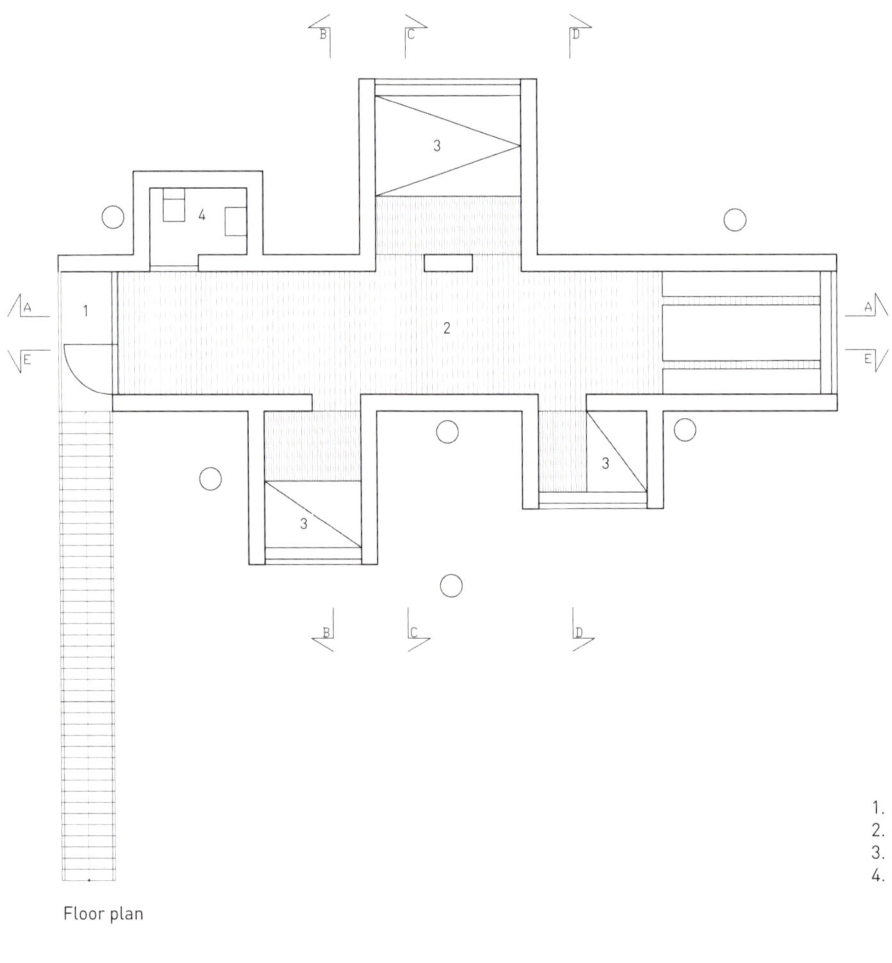

1. Entry / terrace
2. Living room
3. Bedroom 2 persons
4. Toilet

Floor plan

SAFE & GREEN HOLDINGS CORP

Steve Armstrong

Safe & Green Holdings Corp. is a leading developer, designer, and fabricator of modular structures, meeting the growing demand for safe and green construction. The firm offers a product that exceeds many standard building code requirements, and also supports developers, architects, builders and owners in achieving faster execution, greener construction, and buildings of higher value. The Company creates purpose built, pre-fabricated modules from wood, steel, and shipping containers into supreme structures.

Safe & Green Holdings Corp. ist ein führender Entwickler, Konstrukteur und Hersteller von modularen Strukturen und reagiert damit auf die wachsende Nachfrage nach sicheren und umweltfreundlichen Konstruktionen. Das Unternehmen bietet ein Produkt an, das viele Standardanforderungen der Bauvorschriften übertrifft und darüber hinaus Entwicklern, Architekten, Bauherren und Eigentümern hilft, eine schnellere Ausführung, eine umweltfreundlichere Konstruktion und höherwertige Gebäude zu erreichen. Das Unternehmen stellt vorgefertigte Module aus Holz, Stahl und Schiffscontainern zu höchsten Strukturen zusammen.

Safe & Green Holdings Corp. est un leader dans le développement, la conception et la fabrication de structures modulaires, répondant à la demande croissante de constructions sûres et respectueuses de l'environnement. L'entreprise propose un produit qui dépasse de nombreuses exigences du code du bâtiment standard et aide également les promoteurs, les architectes, les constructeurs et les propriétaires à obtenir une exécution plus rapide, une construction plus écologique et des bâtiments de plus grande valeur. L'entreprise crée des modules préfabriqués à partir de bois, d'acier et de conteneurs maritimes pour en faire des structures suprêmes.

Safe & Green Holdings Corp. es una empresa líder en el desarrollo, diseño y fabricación de estructuras modulares, que responde a la creciente demanda de una construcción segura y ecológica. La empresa ofrece un producto que supera muchos de los requisitos de los códigos de construcción estándar, y también ayuda a promotores, arquitectos, constructores y propietarios a conseguir una ejecución más rápida, una construcción más ecológica y edificios de mayor valor. La empresa crea módulos prefabricados a partir de madera, acero y contenedores de transporte en estructuras supremas.

www.safeandgreenholdings.com

1932

THE BEACH BOX

Napeague, New York, United States | Photos: © Lena Yaremenko, Marshall Watson

The Beach Box is a modern, eco-lux container home located in the Sand Dunes of Napeague just moments (900 feet) to ocean beach. The home offers 4 bedrooms and 2.5 bathrooms, 1,300 square feet of exterior decking, plus a new water view roof deck, outdoor shower, and heated pool. All of the aforementioned is wrapped in sleek, eco-conscious design and finishes, including a custom chefs kitchen, stainless touches, EcoTop counters, white washed white oak floors, Cyprus siding and cedar decking all certified sustainable. The tank-less/instantaneous water heating system and central HVAC units were installed for maximum energy efficiency. All appliances are energy star for the highest, most efficient energy performance. The Beach Box is the Hampton's very first eco-container home. The house features amazing views of Napeague Harbor as well as beautiful vistas across acres of dune preserve to the Ocean.

Die Beach Box ist ein modernes, luxuriöses und umweltfreundliches Containerhaus in den Napeague Sanddünen, nur wenige Minuten vom Strand entfernt. Das Haus bietet 4 Schlafzimmer, 2,5 Bäder und 120 m² Außenterrasse, plus eine neue Terrasse mit Blick auf das Wasser, Außendusche und beheizten Pool. All dies ist in ein elegantes, umweltbewusstes Design verpackt, einschließlich einer maßgefertigten Industrieküche, rostfreiem Stahl, EcoTop-Theken, weiß gewaschenen Eichenböden, Zypern-Holzverkleidungen und zertifizierten nachhaltigen Zedernholzdielen. Für maximale Energieeffizienz wurden ein Warmwasser-Durchlauferhitzer und eine zentrale Heizungs- und Lüftungsanlage installiert. Alle Geräte tragen das Energy-Star-Siegel für eine höhere und effizientere Energieleistung. Die Beach Box ist das erste grüne Haus in Hampton. Das Haus bietet eine unglaubliche Aussicht auf den Hafen von Napeague sowie einen wunderschönen Blick über das Dünengebiet bis hin zum Meer.

The Beach Box est une maison moderne, luxueuse et écologique située sur les dunes de sable de Napeague, à quelques minutes de la plage de l'océan. La maison offre 4 chambres, 2,5 salles de bains et 120 m² de terrasse extérieure, plus une nouvelle terrasse avec vue sur l'eau, une douche extérieure et une piscine chauffée. Tout cela est enveloppé dans un design élégant et écologique, comprenant une cuisine industrielle sur mesure, des touches d'acier inoxydable, des comptoirs EcoTop, des sols en chêne blanc lavé, un revêtement en bois de Chypre et une terrasse en cèdre certifié durable. Un système de chauffage de l'eau Tankless/instantané et des unités centrales de CVC ont été installés pour une efficacité énergétique maximale. Tous les appareils sont labellisés Energy Star pour des performances énergétiques supérieures et plus efficaces. La Beach Box est la première maison écologique de Hampton. La maison offre des vues incroyables sur le port de Napeague ainsi que des vues magnifiques sur des hectares de dunes préservées jusqu'à l'océan.

The Beach Box es una moderna casa ecológica de contenedores de lujo situada en las Dunas de Arena de Napeague, a sólo unos minutos de la playa del océano. La casa ofrece 4 dormitorios, 2,5 baños y 120 m² de cubierta exterior, además de una nueva cubierta con vistas al agua, ducha exterior y piscina climatizada. Todo lo anterior está envuelto en un diseño elegante, eco-consciente, incluyendo una cocina industrial a medida, toques de acero inoxidable, contadores EcoTop, suelos de roble blanco lavado, revestimiento de madera de Chipre y cubierta de cedro certificado y sostenible. El sistema de calentamiento de agua sin tanque/instantáneo y las unidades centrales de HVAC se instalaron para una máxima eficiencia energética. Todos los electrodomésticos son de la marca Energy Star para un rendimiento energético más alto y eficiente. The Beach Box es la primera casa ecológica de Hampton. La casa cuenta con increíbles vistas del puerto de Napeague, así como hermosas vistas a través de hectáreas de reserva de dunas hasta el océano.

CHIHULY

CHIHULY

SVA ARCHITECTS, INC.

Robert M. Simons, Ernesto M. Vasquez

SVA Architects, Inc. was founded by Robert M. Simons, AIA, and Ernesto M. Vasquez, FAIA, in 2003. Our innovative and sustainable architectural design and planning services have enhanced educational, residential, work, and public spaces. Our vision begins by understanding the client's needs and desires and proceeds outward to the built and natural environment. We believe these human-scale solutions are the foundation to comprehensive designs that transform our communities.

SVA Architects, Inc. wurde 2003 von Robert M. Simons, AIA, und Ernesto M. Vasquez, FAIA, gegründet. Unsere innovativen und nachhaltigen architektonischen Design- und Planungsleistungen haben Bildungs-, Wohn-, Arbeitsplatz- und öffentliche Räume verbessert. Unsere Vision beginnt mit dem Verständnis für die Bedürfnisse und Wünsche des Kunden und erstreckt sich auf die gebaute und natürliche Umwelt. Wir sind davon überzeugt, dass diese maßstabsgetreuen Lösungen die Grundlage

SVA Architects, Inc. a été fondé par Robert M. Simons, AIA, et Ernesto M. Vasquez, FAIA, en 2003. Nos services de conception architecturale et de planification innovants et durables ont permis d'améliorer les espaces éducatifs, résidentiels, professionnels et publics. Notre vision commence par la compréhension des besoins et des désirs du client et s'étend à l'environnement bâti et naturel. Nous pensons que ces solutions à l'échelle humaine sont le fondement de conceptions globales qui transforment nos

SVA Architects, Inc. fue fundada por Robert M. Simons, AIA, y Ernesto M. Vasquez, FAIA, en 2003. Nuestros servicios de diseño arquitectónico y planificación innovadores y sostenibles han mejorado espacios educativos, residenciales, laborales y públicos. Nuestra visión comienza por comprender las necesidades y deseos del cliente y se extiende al entorno construido y natural. Creemos que estas soluciones a escala humana son la base de diseños integrales que transforman nuestras comu-

POTTER'S LANE PROJECT LOCATION

Midway City, California, U.S.A. | Photos: © Robert A. Hansen

Potter's Lane is a visionary housing project for unhoused military veterans. Modified-steel shipping containers were transformed into fully functional and aesthetically pleasing housing units that harmonize with the surrounding environment. The prefabrication process halved the typical construction schedule. Three standard 20' long steel containers were assembled to form the open-plan units of approximately 450 SF each. The community is composed of 16 units: 15 accommodate previously unhoused veterans with the remaining one housing an onsite manager. Residents can take advantage of onsite services, such as group and individual counseling, medical care, veterans' liaisons, and employment programs.

The unorthodox design reflects the possibilities for sustainability and energy-efficiency while reducing normal development costs and inefficiencies. Potter's Lane seeks to address the issues with homelessness and veteran mental health by giving them the stability they need to get back on their feet.

Potter's Lane ist ein visionäres Wohnprojekt für obdachlose Militärveteranen. Modifizierte Stahlcontainer wurden in voll funktionsfähige und ästhetisch ansprechende Häuser verwandelt, die mit ihrer Umgebung harmonieren. Der Vorfertigungsprozess halbierte die übliche Bauzeit. Drei Standard-Stahlcontainer mit einer Länge von 20 Fuß wurden zu offenen Einheiten von jeweils etwa 450 Quadratmetern zusammengebaut. Die Gemeinschaft besteht aus 16 Wohneinheiten: 15 beherbergen obdachlose Veteranen und die verbleibende Einheit beherbergt einen Manager vor Ort. Die Bewohner können Dienstleistungen wie Gruppen- und Einzelberatung, medizinische Versorgung und Kontakte zu Veteranen und Beschäftigungsprogrammen in Anspruch nehmen.

Das unorthodoxe Design spiegelt die Möglichkeiten von Nachhaltigkeit und Energieeffizienz wider und reduziert gleichzeitig die üblichen Kosten und Ineffizienzen der Entwicklung. Potter's Lane will Obdachlosigkeit und psychische Probleme von Veteranen bekämpfen, indem es ihnen die Stabilität bietet, die sie brauchen, um wieder auf die Beine zu kommen.

Potter's Lane est un projet de logement visionnaire pour les vétérans militaires sans abri. Des conteneurs en acier modifiés ont été transformés en maisons entièrement fonctionnelles et esthétiques qui s'harmonisent avec leur environnement. Le processus de préfabrication a permis de réduire de moitié le temps de construction habituel. Trois conteneurs en acier standard de 20 pieds de long ont été assemblés pour former les unités à plan ouvert d'environ 450 pieds carrés chacune. La communauté se compose de 16 unités : 15 abritent des vétérans sans abri et l'unité restante abrite un gestionnaire sur place. Les résidents peuvent bénéficier de services tels que des conseils collectifs et individuels, des soins médicaux et une liaison avec les anciens combattants et les programmes d'emploi.

La conception peu orthodoxe reflète les possibilités de durabilité et d'efficacité énergétique, tout en réduisant les coûts normaux et les inefficacités du développement. Potter's Lane vise à lutter contre le sans-abrisme et les problèmes de santé mentale des anciens combattants en leur offrant la stabilité dont ils ont besoin pour se remettre sur pied.

Potter's Lane es un visionario proyecto de viviendas para veteranos militares sin hogar. Los contenedores de acero modificado se transformaron en viviendas totalmente funcionales y estéticamente agradables que armonizan con el entorno. El proceso de prefabricación redujo a la mitad el plazo de construcción habitual. Se ensamblaron tres contenedores de acero estándar de 20 pies de largo para formar las unidades de planta abierta de aproximadamente 450 pies cuadrados cada una. La comunidad se compone de 16 unidades: 15 alojan a veteranos sin vivienda y la restante a un gestor in situ. Los residentes pueden beneficiarse de servicios como el asesoramiento grupal e individual, la atención médica, y el enlace con veteranos y programas de empleo.

El diseño poco ortodoxo refleja las posibilidades de sostenibilidad y eficiencia energética, al tiempo que reduce los costes e ineficiencias normales del desarrollo. Potter's Lane pretende abordar los problemas de las personas sin hogar y la salud mental de los veteranos ofreciéndoles la estabilidad que necesitan para volver a ponerse en pie.

POTTERS LANE
15171 JACKSON STREET

Budget
Budget
15161

TRA | THOMAS ROSZAK ARCHITECTURE

THOMAS ROSZAK

Thomas Roszak (1966, Chicago) is an American architect, real estate developer, author, and academic. Roszak received a B.Arch from the Illinois Institute of Technology (IIT) in 1989. He founded and leads four companies: Thomas Roszak Architecture, SteelGrass Construction Management, TR Management+-Consulting, and Moceri+Roszak Development. He has designed and developed projects representing more than $3 billion in the Chicago area. He was an Adjunct Professor at the IIT College of Architecture. In 2020, Roszak was elevated to a Fellow (FAIA) of the American Institute of Architects.

Thomas Roszak (1966, Chicago) ist ein amerikanischer Architekt, Immobilienentwickler, Autor und Wissenschaftler. Roszak erwarb 1989 einen B.Arch. am Illinois Institute of Technology (IIT). Er gründete und leitet vier Unternehmen: Thomas Roszak Architecture, SteelGrass Construction Management, TR Management+Consulting, und Moceri+Roszak Development. Er hat im Großraum Chicago Projekte im Wert von mehr als 3 Milliarden Dollar entworfen und entwickelt. Er war Adjunct Professor am IIT College of Architecture. Im Jahr 2020 wurde Roszak zum Fellow (FAIA) des American Institute of Architects ernannt.

Thomas Roszak (1966, Chicago) est un architecte, promoteur immobilier, auteur et universitaire américain. Roszak a obtenu un B.Arch de l'Illinois Institute of Technology (IIT) en 1989. Il a fondé et dirige quatre entreprises : Thomas Roszak Architecture, SteelGrass Construction Management, TR Management+Consulting, et Moceri+Roszak Development. Il a conçu et développé des projets représentant plus de 3 milliards de dollars dans la région de Chicago. Il a été professeur auxiliaire à l'école d'architecture de l'IIT. En 2020, Roszak a été élevé au rang de Fellow (FAIA) de l'American Institute of Architects.

Thomas Roszak (1966, Chicago) es un arquitecto, promotor inmobiliario, autor y académico estadounidense. Roszak se licenció en Arquitectura por el Instituto Tecnológico de Illinois (IIT) en 1989. Fundó y dirige cuatro empresas: Thomas Roszak Architecture, SteelGrass Construction Management, TR Management+Consulting y Moceri+Roszak Development. Ha diseñado y desarrollado proyectos que representan más de 3.000 millones de dólares en el área de Chicago. Fue profesor adjunto en la Escuela de Arquitectura del IIT. En 2020, Roszak fue elevado a miembro (FAIA) del Instituto Americano de Arquitectos.

www.roszak.com

RECES

CITY HALL

RECESS AND CITY HALL EVENTS

Chicago, Illinois, United States | Photos: © Sean Henderson

This adaptive re-use project converted two former abandoned factories built in the early 20th century and an adjacent surface parking lot into a 30,000-square-foot entertainment complex with 15,500 square feet of indoor event and restaurant space and a 14,500-square-foot open-air courtyard dining terrace.

The plan integrates two industrial buildings into a cohesive whole. New factory-style windows provide daylight as well as views of the Chicago skyline. Repurposed doors, boilers, and steel beams have been re-imagined as artwork, evoking the historic industrial aesthetic of the original buildings. On the west end of the site the architects transformed an empty parking lot into a lively outdoor terrace by surrounding it with 30 recycled shipping containers. The redevelopment improves the public realm and upholds the urban fabric by repurposing vacant facilities into a contemporary, bustling place for entertainment, enhancing the work-live-play needs.

Bei diesem Projekt wurden zwei ehemalige, im frühen 20. Jahrhundert errichtete, verlassene Fabriken und ein angrenzender oberirdischer Parkplatz in einen 3.000 m^2 großen Unterhaltungskomplex mit 1.500 m^2 Innenfläche für Veranstaltungen und Restaurants und einer 1.450 m^2 großen Terrasse für Mahlzeiten im Freien umgewandelt.

Der Plan integriert zwei Industriegebäude in ein zusammenhängendes Ganzes. Neue Fenster im Fabrikstil sorgen für Tageslicht und geben den Blick auf die Skyline von Chicago frei. Wiederverwendete Türen, Heizkessel und Stahlträger wurden als Kunstwerke neu gestaltet und erinnern an die historische Industrieästhetik der ursprünglichen Gebäude. Am westlichen Ende des Geländes verwandelten die Architekten einen leeren Parkplatz in eine lebendige Außenterrasse, indem sie ihn mit 30 recycelten Schiffscontainern umgaben. Die Sanierung verbessert den öffentlichen Raum und erhält das städtische Gefüge, indem leerstehende Gebäude in einen modernen, belebten Ort der Unterhaltung umgewandelt werden, der die Bedürfnisse von Arbeit, Leben und Freizeit erfüllt.

Ce projet de réutilisation adaptative a converti deux anciennes usines abandonnées construites au début du 20e siècle et un parking de surface adjacent en un complexe de divertissement de 3.000 m^2 avec 1.500 m^2 d'espace intérieur pour les événements et les restaurants et une terrasse de 1.450 m^2 pour les repas dans une cour en plein air.

Le plan intègre deux bâtiments industriels dans un ensemble cohérent. De nouvelles fenêtres de style industriel laissent passer la lumière du jour et offrent une vue sur la ligne d'horizon de Chicago. Des portes, des chaudières et des poutres d'acier réutilisées ont été réimaginées en œuvres d'art, évoquant l'esthétique industrielle historique des bâtiments d'origine. À l'extrémité ouest du site, les architectes ont transformé un parking vide en une terrasse extérieure animée en l'entourant de 30 conteneurs d'expédition recyclés. Le réaménagement améliore le domaine public et maintient le tissu urbain en réaffectant des installations vacantes en un lieu de divertissement contemporain et animé, qui répond aux besoins de travailler, vivre et jouer.

Este proyecto de reutilización adaptativa convirtió dos antiguas fábricas abandonadas construidas a principios del siglo XX y un aparcamiento de superficie adyacente en un complejo de ocio de 3.000 m^2 con 1.500 m^2 de espacio interior para eventos y restaurantes y una terraza comedor de 1.450 m^2 al aire libre.

El plan integra dos edificios industriales en un todo cohesionado. Las nuevas ventanas de estilo industrial proporcionan luz natural y vistas del horizonte de Chicago. Las puertas, las calderas y las vigas de acero reutilizadas se han reinterpretado como obras de arte, evocando la estética industrial histórica de los edificios originales. En el extremo oeste del solar, los arquitectos transformaron un aparcamiento vacío en una animada terraza al aire libre, rodeándolo con 30 contenedores de transporte reciclados. La remodelación mejora el espacio público y mantiene el tejido urbano al reutilizar las instalaciones vacías para convertirlas en un lugar de ocio contemporáneo y animado, mejorando las necesidades de trabajo-vida-juego.

XINES
CAPITAL
msc

msc
msc

COSCO
RECESS

MAERSK

CBHU 363683
2261
MGW.
TARE.
CU. CAP.
AERSK

MAERS

TOILETTES

TOILETTES

TRAVIS PRICE ARCHITECTS

Travis Price, Kelly Davies Grace

Travis Price, FAIA, is an architect, author, professor, and philosopher with four decades of groundbreaking design to his name. He lectures on and creates modern architecture informed by ecology and mythology. His award-winning projects include residential, commercial, and institutional designs. In 2019, he was nominated for the coveted AIA Gold Medal for his historic contributions to "ecological and cultural literacy in modern architecture."
Kelly Davies Grace, AIA is an award winning senior architect at TPA and Managing Partner of KGPBuild Inc Construction.

Travis Price, FAIA, ist Architekt, Autor, Lehrer und Philosoph mit vier Jahrzehnten Erfahrung in innovativem Design. Er hält Vorträge und entwirft moderne Architektur auf der Grundlage von Ökologie und Mythologie. Zu seinen preisgekrönten Projekten gehören Entwürfe für Wohnhäuser, Unternehmen und Institutionen. 2019 wurde er für die begehrte AIA-Goldmedaille für seine historischen Beiträge zur „ökologischen und kulturellen Bildung in der modernen Architektur" nominiert.
Kelly Davies Grace, AIA, ist eine preisgekrönte leitende Architektin bei TPA und geschäftsführende Gesellschafterin von KGPBuild Inc Construction.

Travis Price, FAIA, est un architecte, un auteur, un enseignant et un philosophe qui possède quatre décennies d'expérience en matière de conception innovante. Il donne des conférences et crée une architecture moderne basée sur l'écologie et la mythologie. Ses projets primés comprennent des conceptions résidentielles, commerciales et institutionnelles. En 2019, il a été nommé pour la très convoitée médaille d'or de l'AIA pour ses contributions historiques à la « littératie écologique et culturelle dans l'architecture moderne. »
Kelly Davies Grace, AIA, est un architecte principal primé de TPA et associé directeur de KGPBuild Inc Construction.

Travis Price, FAIA, es un arquitecto, autor, profesor y filósofo con cuatro décadas de experiencia de diseño innovador. Da conferencias y crea una arquitectura moderna basada en la ecología y la mitología. Sus proyectos premiados incluyen diseños residenciales, comerciales e institucionales. En 2019, fue nominado para la codiciada Medalla de Oro de la AIA por sus contribuciones históricas a la «alfabetización ecológica y cultural en la arquitectura moderna.»
Kelly Davies Grace, AIA es un galardonado arquitecto senior en TPA y socio gerente de KGPBuild Inc Construction.

www.travispricearchitects.com

AARON POMERANTZ BACK YD

Washington DC, United States | Photos: © Ken Wyner

Aaron Pomerantz is a major DC real estate broker by trade. More so he is a lover of art, architecture, and artists. (Architects too!) Aaron and his wife Irina also needed more space in their Washington DC townhouse packed with art. The simple one container gallery fit perfectly in their back yard, literally within inches of the highly restricted "back yard" footprint allowances for an accessory addition in DC. The design intention was a floating art gallery in the garden for his collections and his gala sales parties for his artists. The clean white paint canvas. and the glass bump outs made a great walk thorough inside and around the gallery. The container was singing as an art gallery with art itself both indoors and outdoors. However, it was literally hell on wheels the day of delivery. The snow was over a foot deep and the crane had to become a gargantuan caterpillar wiggling down the chaotic back alleys with an HGTV film crew to boot. The project was a major DC breakthrough with huge support from the city's leadership. Phase II was planned to add yet another floor on top. It has been permitted and will be completed in early 2023! Cranes away, the city is now on fire with back yard container elegance!

Aaron Pomerantz ist ein führender Immobilienmakler sowie ein Liebhaber von Kunst, Architektur und Künstlern (auch Architekten!). Aaron und seine Frau Irina brauchten mehr Platz in ihrem mit Kunst gefüllten Stadthaus in Washington DC. Die einfache Galerie in Form eines Anbaus passte perfekt in ihren Hinterhof. Das Konzept besteht aus einer schwimmenden Kunstgalerie im Garten für ihre Sammlungen und Gala-Partys für ihre Künstler. Die weiß gestrichene Leinwand und die Glasleisten sorgten für einen großartigen Rundgang innerhalb und außerhalb der Galerie. Der Tag der Lieferung war jedoch buchstäblich die Hölle auf Rädern. Bei einer Schneehöhe von über 30 cm musste sich der Kran in eine riesige Raupe verwandeln, die sich in Begleitung eines HGTV-Filmteams durch die chaotischen Gassen bewegte. Das Projekt war ein großer Durchbruch in Washington DC und wurde von der Stadtverwaltung nachdrücklich unterstützt. In einer zweiten Phase sollte ein zusätzliches Stockwerk aufgesetzt werden, das nun genehmigt wurde und Anfang 2023 fertiggestellt werden soll. Jetzt, wo die Kräne verschwunden sind, freut sich die Stadt über die Eleganz dieser in Hinterhöfen gebauten Container.

Aaron Pomerantz est un agent immobilier de premier plan, ainsi qu'un amoureux de l'art, de l'architecture et des artistes (des architectes aussi !). Aaron et sa femme Irina avaient besoin de plus d'espace dans leur maison de ville de Washington DC, remplie d'art. La galerie simple, sous forme d'annexe, s'est parfaitement intégrée dans leur jardin. Le concept consiste en une galerie d'art flottante dans le jardin pour leurs collections et des fêtes de gala pour leurs artistes. La toile peinte en blanc et les rebords en verre ont permis une grande promenade à l'intérieur et à l'extérieur de la galerie. Cependant, le jour de la livraison a été littéralement un enfer sur roues. Avec une hauteur de neige de plus de 30 cm, la grue a dû se transformer en une chenille géante se déplaçant dans les ruelles chaotiques, accompagnée d'une équipe de tournage de HGTV. Le projet a fait une percée majeure à Washington DC, avec un fort soutien des dirigeants de la ville. Une deuxième phase était prévue pour ajouter un étage supplémentaire au dessus, qui a maintenant été autorisée et sera achevée au début de 2023. Les grues ayant disparu, la ville se réjouit désormais de l'élégance de ces conteneurs construits dans les arrière-cours.

Aaron Pomerantz es un importante agente inmobiliario, además de amante del arte, de la arquitectura y de los artistas (¡Los arquitectos también!). Aaron y su esposa Irina necesitaban más espacio en su casa adosada de Washington DC repleta de arte. La sencilla galería, en forma de anexo, encajaba perfectamente en su patio trasero. El concepto consiste en una galería de arte flotante en el jardín para sus colecciones y sus fiestas de gala para sus artistas. El lienzo de pintura blanca y los salientes de vidrio consiguieron un gran paseo a través del interior y exterior de la galería. Sin embargo, el dia de la entrega fue literalmente un infierno sobre ruedas. Con nieve por encima de los 30 cm de altura, la grúa tuvo que convertirse en una oruga gigantesca que se movía por los caóticos callejones acompañada de un equipo de filmación de HGTV. El proyecto supuso un gran avance en Washington DC, con un gran apoyo de los dirigentes de la ciudad. Se planeó la segunda fase para añadir una planta más en la parte superior que ya ha sido autorizada y que se completará a principios de 2023. Con las grúas ya fuera, la ciudad está ahora encantada con la elegancia de estos contenedores construidos en patios traseros.

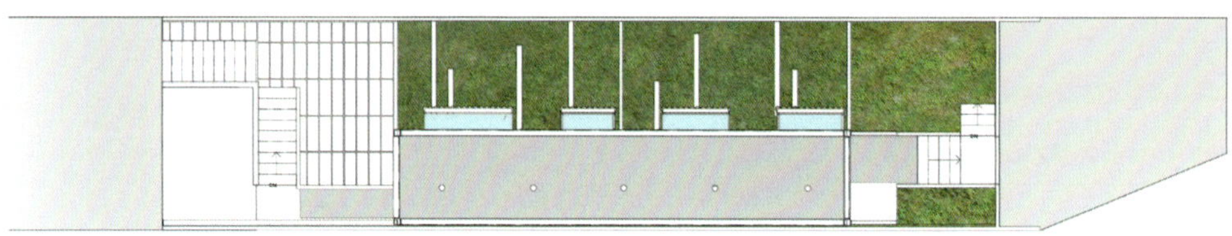

Site plan

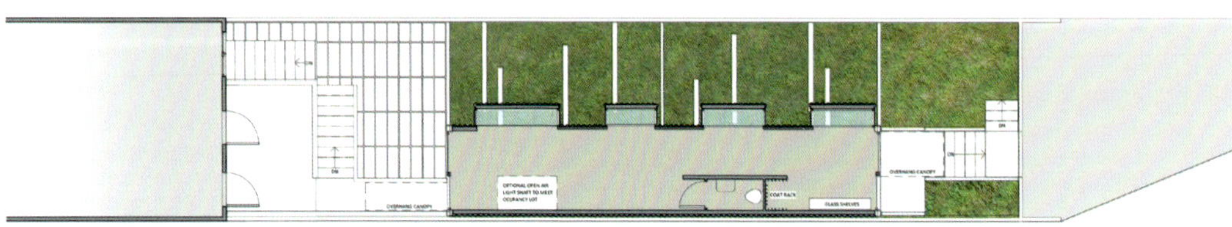

First floor plan

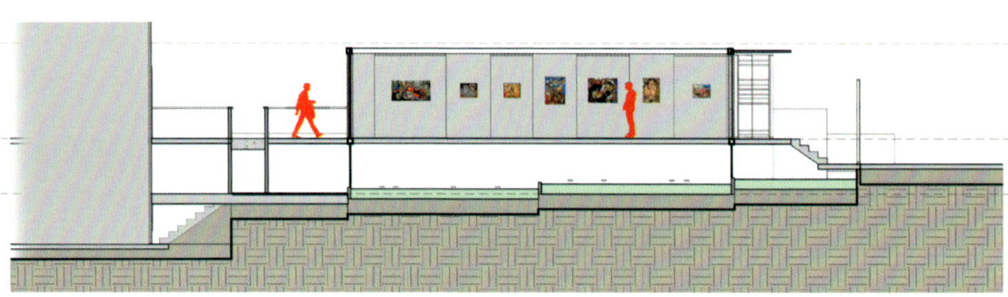

Section

ARUN ARUMUGASWAMY & ARCHANA INKU SHAH RESIDENCE

Silver Spring, Maryland, United States | Photos: © Dan Westergren

The site was a rare find inside the beltway along the flowing Sligo Creek on a high cliff abutting Washington, DC. The clients were in love with Sea Container modernism. Indeed airplanes, cars and more were a big part of Arun's life and passion. The elegant simplicity was a keen element for both Arun and Archana and their new twin wee ones. Looking over the creek in a well-wooded neighborhood was magnificent. The design construction is a simple 4-sea container-hybrid. The home is constructed with 4 - 8'x40'x9'6" tall sea containers split apart. A two-story living room 20 ft wide is a simple TJI span. The entire home sits on a concrete basement/foundation with an attached workshop/garage. The second floor has access to a green roof food garden well away from the never-ending deer/rabbit invaders. The use of extended steel/glass "bump-outs" added the key ingredients to widen the container rooms with views left, right, and skyward. Most of the landscape was fully preserved as well as existing highly regulated eco storm water management hardscapes. The design lyric was the elegant simplicity of modern repurposed metals that celebrate the flight of a pilot and the serenity of a healer. In concert, the design created unexpected sky views floating over the soft treetops and the cascading stream.

Der Standort war ein seltener Fund innerhalb der Umgehungsstraße, entlang des fließenden Sligo Creek, auf einer hohen Klippe an der Grenze zu Washington, DC. Die Kunden waren von der Modernität der Schiffscontainer angetan. In der Tat waren Flugzeuge, Autos usw. Teil von Aruns Leben und seiner Leidenschaft. Die elegante Einfachheit war ein Element, das sowohl von Arun und Archana als auch von ihren neuen Zwillingen sehr geschätzt wurde. Der Blick über den Bach in einer waldreichen Umgebung war herrlich. Die Konstruktion des Entwurfs ist ein einfacher Container-Hybrid. Das Haus ist auf der Basis von 4 separaten 8'x40'x9'6" hohen Schiffscontainern mit einem 20' breiten zweistöckigen Wohnzimmer gebaut. Das gesamte Haus steht auf einem Betonkeller/Fundament mit einer angeschlossenen Werkstatt/Garage. Das erste Stockwerk hat Zugang zu einem begrünten Dachgemüsegarten, weit weg von den eindringenden Rehen und Kaninchen. Die Verwendung von erweiterten Stahl-/Glas-„Bump-Outs" trug wesentlich dazu bei, die Containerräume mit Blicken nach links, rechts und in den Himmel zu erweitern. Ein großer Teil der Landschaft wurde vollständig erhalten, ebenso wie die stark regulierte Regenwasserbewirtschaftung. Die Lyrik des Designs basiert auf der eleganten Einfachheit moderner wiederverwendeter Metalle, die den Flug eines Piloten und die Gelassenheit eines Heilers zelebrieren. Insgesamt schuf das Design unerwartete Ausblicke auf den Himmel, der über den sanften Baumkronen und dem kaskadenförmigen Bachlauf schwebt.

Le site était une trouvaille rare à l'intérieur du périphérique, le long de la rivière Sligo Creek, sur une falaise élevée jouxtant Washington, DC. Les clients ont été séduits par le modernisme des conteneurs maritimes. En effet, les avions, les voitures, etc. faisaient partie de la vie et de la passion d'Arun. La simplicité élégante était un élément très apprécié par Arun et Archana et leurs nouveaux jumeaux. La vue sur le ruisseau dans un quartier bien boisé était magnifique. La construction de la conception est un simple conteneur-hybride. La maison est construite sur la base de 4 conteneurs d'expédition séparés de 8'x40'x9'6" de haut avec un salon de 20' de large sur deux étages. La maison entière repose sur un sous-sol/fondation en béton avec un atelier/garage attenant. Le premier étage donne accès à un jardin potager sur le toit, à l'abri des cerfs et des lapins. L'utilisation d'avancées en acier et en verre a permis de prolonger les pièces du conteneur avec des vues sur la gauche, la droite et le ciel. Une grande partie de l'aménagement paysager a été conservée dans son intégralité, de même que les revêtements durs de gestion des eaux pluviales très réglementés. Le lyrisme du design repose sur l'élégante simplicité des métaux modernes réutilisés qui célèbrent le vol d'un pilote et la sérénité d'un guérisseur. Dans l'ensemble, la conception a créé des vues inattendues du ciel flottant au-dessus des cimes douces des arbres et du ruisseau en cascade.

El emplazamiento era un raro hallazgo dentro de la circunvalación, a lo largo del caudaloso Sligo Creek, en un alto acantilado colindante con Washington, DC. Los clientes estaban enamorados del modernismo de los contenedores marítimos. De hecho, los aviones, los coches y demás formaban parte de la vida y la pasión de Arun. La elegante sencillez fue un elemento muy apreciado tanto por Arun y Archana como por sus nuevos gemelos. La vista sobre el arroyo en un barrio bien arbolado era magnífica. La construcción del diseño es un simple contenedor-híbrido. La casa está construida en base a 4 contenedores marítimos separados de 8'x40'x9'6" de altura con una sala de estar de dos pisos de 20 pies de ancho. Toda la casa se asienta sobre un sótano/fundación de hormigón con un taller/garaje adjunto. El segundo piso tiene acceso a un huerto en el techo verde bien lejos de los invasores de ciervos y conejos. El uso de «bump-outs» extendidos de acero/vidrio añadió los ingredientes clave para ampliar las salas de contenedores con vistas a la izquierda, a la derecha y al cielo. La mayor parte del paisaje se conservó íntegramente, así como los paisajes duros de gestión de aguas pluviales, altamente regulados. La lírica del diseño se basó en la elegante simplicidad de los modernos metales reutilizados que celebran el vuelo de un piloto y la serenidad de un sanador. En conjunto, el diseño creó unas inesperadas vistas del cielo flotando sobre las suaves copas de los árboles y el arroyo en cascada.

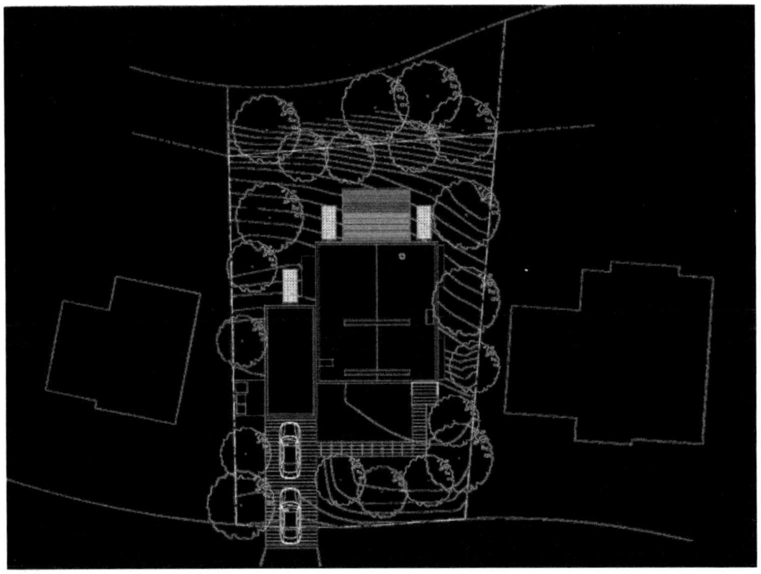

Site plan

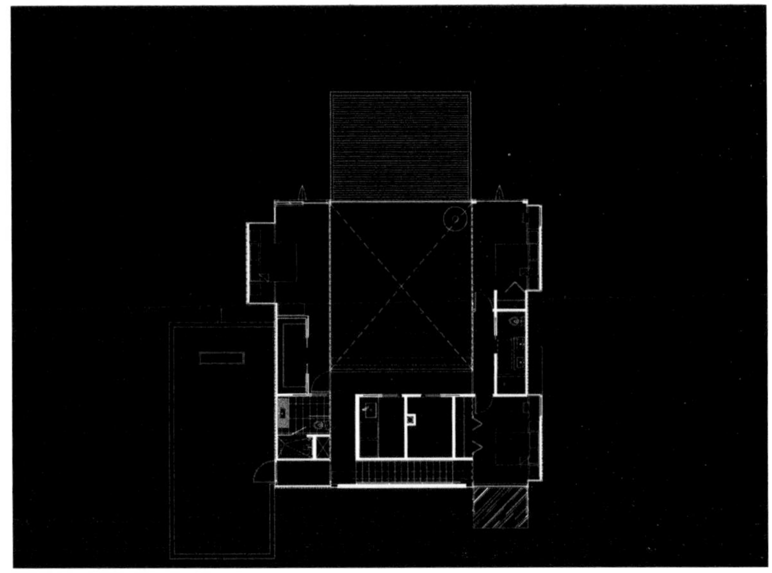

Second floor plan

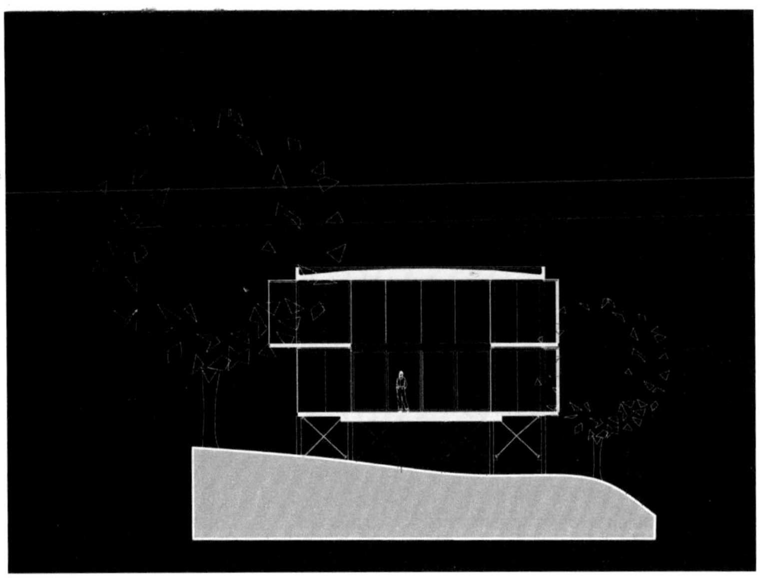

Side to side section

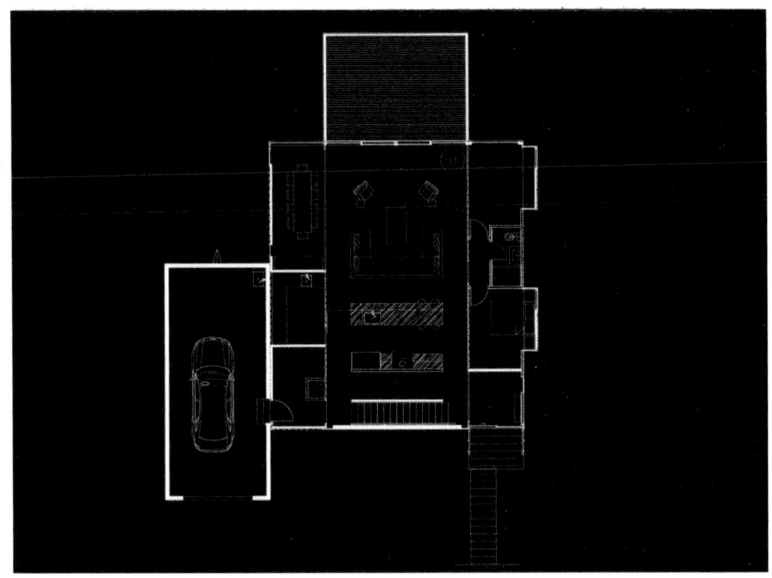

First floor plan

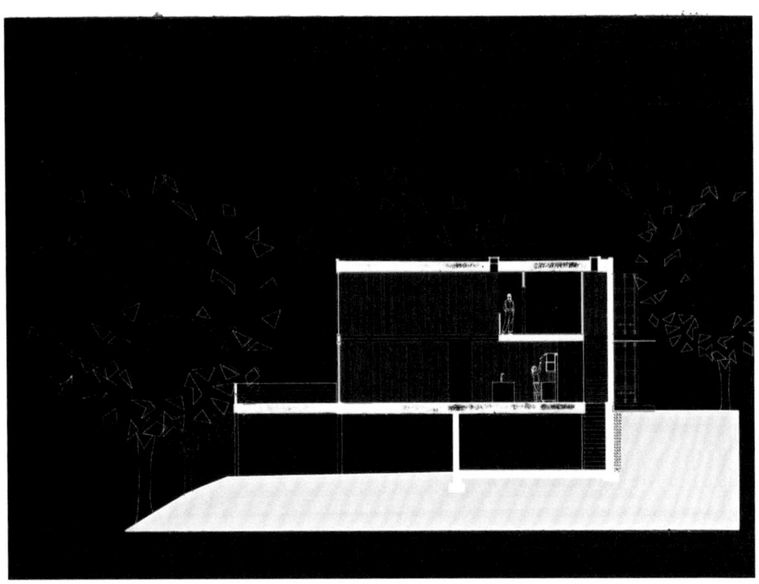

Front to back section

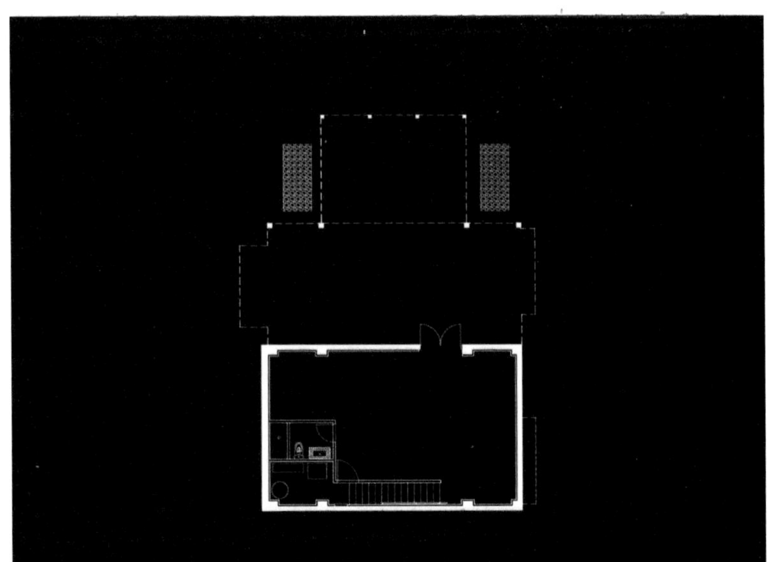

Basement plan

BROOKLAND SEAUA APTS

Washington DC, United States | Photos: Travis Price Architects, Inc

It was our first project with sea containers. The design stacked simply to best fit the site, and the budget. The ground floor started half underground to match zoning height restrictions. It was an insulated concrete wall with 6 bedrooms and a bath for each. Also, a large common area per floor included a shared kitchen, dining, and living room. The same floor plan continued above for 3 more floors using 18 - 8'x40' sea containers. A large highly insulated and translucent wall lit up the interiors on both sides. The ends of each floor were the bedrooms. It was a simple, elegant and expeditious design.

The interiors were maple plywood walls for warmth and ease maintenance. The wood container floors remained refurbished as usual. Inside walls were heavily insulated with beautiful maple wood finishes. We dramatized the handicap ramp to the entry and accommodated the stairway as an indoor translucent design joy.

In DC, the process of building permits alone is exceedingly painful, usually taking 9 months at a minimum! However, with heavy daily construction loads, the project was literally approved, built and occupied within 7 months, going viral in the US and globally.

Dies war unser erstes Seecontainer-Projekt. Das Design wurde einfach gestapelt, um dem Standort und dem Budget am besten gerecht zu werden. Das Erdgeschoss wurde halb eingegraben, um den Höhenbeschränkungen des Gebiets gerecht zu werden. Es handelte sich um eine isolierte Betonwand mit 6 Schlafzimmern und jeweils einem Badezimmer. Darüber hinaus gab es auf jeder Etage einen großen Gemeinschaftsraum mit Küche, Esszimmer und Wohnzimmer. Derselbe Plan wurde im Obergeschoss mit 18 8'x40'-Schiffscontainern für 3 weitere Stockwerke fortgesetzt. Eine große lichtdurchlässige und hochisolierende Wand beleuchtete die Innenräume von beiden Seiten. An den Enden jedes Stockwerks befanden sich die Schlafzimmer, wodurch ein einfaches, elegantes und zügiges Design erreicht wurde.

Die Innenräume haben Ahornsperrholzwände für Wärme und einfache Wartung. Die Böden der Holzcontainer blieben wie immer erhalten. Die Innenwände wurden stark isoliert und mit schönem Ahornholz verkleidet. Wir haben die Behindertenrampe am Eingang dramatisiert und die Treppe als lichtdurchlässige Innenraumgestaltung untergebracht.

In DC ist allein das Baugenehmigungsverfahren äußerst mühsam und dauert normalerweise mindestens 9 Monate! Angesichts des hohen täglichen Arbeitsaufkommens wurde das Projekt jedoch buchstäblich in sieben Monaten genehmigt, gebaut und bezogen, was in den USA und auf der ganzen Welt für Aufsehen sorgte.

Il s'agissait de notre premier projet de conteneur maritime. Le design a été simplement empilé pour s'adapter au mieux au site et au budget. Le rez-de-chaussée a commencé par être semi-enterré pour respecter les restrictions de hauteur de la zone. C'était un mur de béton isolé avec 6 chambres et une salle de bain pour chacune. En outre, chaque étage disposait d'un grand espace commun avec cuisine, salle à manger et salon. Le même plan s'est poursuivi à l'étage supérieur pour 3 étages supplémentaires en utilisant 18 conteneurs d'expédition de 8'x40'. Un grand mur translucide et très isolant éclaire les intérieurs des deux côtés. Les chambres à coucher se trouvaient aux extrémités de chaque étage, ce qui a permis d'obtenir un design simple, élégant et rapide.

Les intérieurs ont des parois en contreplaqué d'érable pour la chaleur et la facilité d'entretien. Les sols des conteneurs en bois sont restés les mêmes que d'habitude. Les murs intérieurs ont été fortement isolés avec de belles finitions en bois d'érable. Nous avons mis en valeur la rampe d'accès pour les handicapés à l'entrée et fait de l'escalier une joie intérieure de conception translucide.

À Washington, la procédure d'obtention d'un permis de construire est à elle seule extrêmement pénible et prend généralement au moins 9 mois ! Cependant, avec la lourde charge de construction quotidienne, le projet a été littéralement approuvé, construit et occupé en 7 mois, devenant viral aux États-Unis et dans le monde entier.

Fue nuestro primer proyecto con contenedores marítimos. El diseño se apiló simplemente para adaptarse mejor al emplazamiento y al presupuesto. La planta baja empezó semi enterrada para ajustarse a las restricciones de altura de la zona. Era un muro de hormigón aislado con 6 dormitorios y un baño para cada uno. Además, cada planta tenía una gran zona común con cocina, comedor y sala de estar. El mismo plano continuó en la planta superior durante 3 plantas más utilizando 18 contenedores marítimos de 8'x40'. Una gran pared traslúcida y altamente aislante iluminaba los interiores por ambos lados. Los extremos de cada planta eran los dormitorios, consiguiendo un diseño sencillo, elegante y expeditivo.

Los interiores gozan de paredes de madera contrachapada de arce para dar calidez y facilitar el mantenimiento. Los suelos de los contenedores de madera seguían siendo los de siempre. Las paredes interiores estaban fuertemente aisladas con bellos acabados de madera de arce. Dramatizamos la rampa para minusválidos de la entrada y acomodamos la escalera como una alegría interior de diseño traslúcido.

En DC, el proceso de permisos de construcción por sí solo es excesivamente doloroso, ¡suele llevar 9 meses como mínimo! Sin embargo, con la pesada carga diaria de construcción, el proyecto fue literalmente aprobado, construido y ocupado en 7 meses, convirtiéndose en viral en EE.UU. y en todo el mundo.

EXIT

UDDU DESIGN

Taavi Aunre

Taavi Aunre is a senior interior architect with a unique sense of design and has nearly 30 years of work experience creating various commercial and living spaces. During this time, he has designed more than 1000 projects, including restaurants, nightclubs, offices, shops, service establishments and much more.
Taavi uses versatile design styles and techniques in his work, which have achieved success in developing and implementing ideas for various interior projects.
He is a highly valued interior designer, recognised in Estonia as a man with excellent functional and practical design skills.

www.uddu.ee

Taavi Aunre ist eine Innenarchitektin mit einem einzigartigen Sinn für Design und fast 30 Jahren Berufserfahrung in der Gestaltung verschiedener Geschäfts- und Wohnräume. In dieser Zeit hat er über 1000 Projekte entworfen, darunter Restaurants, Nachtclubs, Büros, Geschäfte, Dienstleistungseinrichtungen und vieles mehr.
Taavi verwendet in seiner Arbeit vielseitige Designstile und -techniken, mit denen er erfolgreich Ideen für verschiedene Innenraumprojekte entwickelt und umgesetzt hat.
Er ist ein hoch geschätzter Innenarchitekt, der in Estland als Mann mit hervorragenden funktionalen und praktischen Designfähigkeiten anerkannt ist.

Taavi Aunre est un architecte d'intérieur doté d'un sens unique du design et de près de 30 ans d'expérience professionnelle dans la création de divers espaces commerciaux et résidentiels. Pendant cette période, il a conçu plus de 1000 projets, dont des restaurants, des boîtes de nuit, des bureaux, des magasins, des établissements de services et bien plus encore.
Taavi utilise des styles et des techniques de conception polyvalents dans son travail, avec lesquels il a réussi à développer et à mettre en œuvre des idées pour divers projets d'intérieur.
Il est un architecte d'intérieur très apprécié, reconnu en Estonie comme un homme possédant d'excellentes compétences en matière de design fonctionnel et pratique.

Taavi Aunre es un arquitecto de interiores con un sentido único del diseño y casi 30 años de experiencia laboral en la creación de diversos espacios comerciales y residenciales. Durante este tiempo, ha diseñado más de 1000 proyectos, entre restaurantes, clubes nocturnos, oficinas, tiendas, establecimientos de servicios y mucho más.
Taavi utiliza en su trabajo estilos y técnicas de diseño versátiles, con los que ha logrado el éxito en el desarrollo y la aplicación de ideas para diversos proyectos de interiores.
Es un diseñador de interiores muy valorado, reconocido en Estonia como un hombre con excelentes aptitudes para el diseño funcional y práctico.

Hektor
Container

HEKTOR CONTAINER HOTEL

Tallinn, Estonia | Photos: © Kristjan Mõru, Tiina-Liina Uudam, Terje Ugandi

In 2018, the railway depot in Tallinn, Estonia, needed an intense and exciting approach to bring the old depo house back to life.
The original depot building was constructed in 1873-1874; it has a strong history in the local railway industry and needed a fresh idea to impact the local Telliskivi creative neighbourhood and a hotel that in the classical sense would not have fit.
During the process, we decided to change the building and the external appearance of the containers as little as possible. The interior of the containers had to be changed to make them cosy and liveable. For this, we used materials such as natural plywood and wood. The walkways between the containers, the reception floor, and the furniture have a wooden feel. The hotel rooms are warm with neutral lines, and the reception area is accentuated with an industrial style, which fits into the existing historic factory interior.
The hotel's 84 rooms have a queen-size bed with luxury bedding, a work desk, an armchair, 43-inch smart TV and a private bathroom & toilet – comfortable, quiet, and functional rooms with calm Nordic design located inside the shipping containers.

Im Jahr 2018 brauchte das Eisenbahndepot in Tallinn, Estland, einen intensiven und spannenden Ansatz, um das ehemalige Lagerhaus wieder zum Leben zu erwecken.
Das ursprüngliche Gebäude wurde 1873-1874 erbaut; es hat eine lange Geschichte in der lokalen Eisenbahnindustrie und brauchte eine neue Idee, um das lokale kreative Viertel von Telliskivi zu beeinflussen, und ein Hotel, das im klassischen Sinne nicht gepasst hätte.
Dabei haben wir beschlossen, das Gebäude und das äußere Erscheinungsbild der Container so wenig wie möglich zu verändern. Das Innere der Container musste verändert werden, um sie gemütlich und bewohnbar zu machen. Dazu haben wir Materialien wie natürliches Sperrholz verwendet. Die Gänge zwischen den Containern, der Empfangsbereich und die Möbel strahlen Wärme aus. Auch die Hotelzimmer sind warm, mit neutralen Linien. Der Empfangsbereich ist in einem industriellen Stil gehalten, der sich in das historische Interieur der bestehenden Fabrik einfügt.
Die 84 Zimmer des Hotels verfügen über ein Doppelbett mit luxuriöser Bettwäsche, einen Schreibtisch, einen Sessel, einen 43-Zoll-Smart-TV sowie ein eigenes Bad und eine Toilette: komfortable, ruhige und funktionale Zimmer in ruhigem nordischen Design, die sich im Inneren der Schiffscontainer befinden.

En 2018, le dépôt ferroviaire de Tallinn, en Estonie, avait besoin d'une approche intense et passionnante pour redonner vie à l'ancienne maison-entrepôt.
Le bâtiment d'origine a été construit en 1873-1874 ; il a une histoire forte dans l'industrie ferroviaire locale et avait besoin d'une idée nouvelle pour avoir un impact sur le quartier créatif local de Telliskivi et un hôtel qui, au sens classique, n'aurait pas été adapté.
Au cours du processus, nous avons décidé de modifier le moins possible le bâtiment et l'aspect extérieur des conteneurs. L'intérieur des conteneurs a dû être modifié pour les rendre confortables et habitables. Pour ce faire, nous avons utilisé des matériaux tels que le contreplaqué naturel. Les passerelles entre les conteneurs, le sol de la réception et le mobilier ont un air de chaleur. Les chambres de l'hôtel sont également chaleureuses, avec des lignes neutres. La zone de réception est agrémentée d'un style industriel, qui s'intègre à l'intérieur historique de l'usine existante.
Les 84 chambres de l'hôtel disposent d'un lit double avec une literie de luxe, d'un bureau, d'un fauteuil, d'une télévision intelligente de 43 pouces et d'une salle de bains et de toilettes privées : des chambres confortables, calmes et fonctionnelles au design nordique calme situées à l'intérieur des conteneurs d'expédition.

En 2018, el depósito ferroviario de Tallin, Estonia, necesitaba un enfoque intenso y emocionante para devolver la vida a la antigua casa del almacén.
El edificio original se construyó en 1873-1874; tiene una fuerte historia en la industria ferroviaria local y necesitaba una idea fresca para impactar en el barrio creativo local de Telliskivi y un hotel que en el sentido clásico no habría encajado.
Durante el proceso, decidimos cambiar lo menos posible el edificio y el aspecto exterior de los contenedores. Había que cambiar el interior de los contenedores para hacerlos acogedores y habitables. Para ello, utilizamos materiales como la madera contrachapada natural. Las pasarelas entre los contenedores, el suelo de la recepción y el mobiliario tienen un aire de calidez. Las habitaciones del hotel son tambien cálidas, con líneas neutras. La zona de recepción está acentuada con un estilo industrial, que encaja con el interior histórico de la fábrica existente.
Las 84 habitaciones del hotel disponen de cama de matrimonio con ropa de cama de lujo, escritorio, sillón, smart TV de 43 pulgadas y cuarto de baño y aseo privados: habitaciones cómodas, tranquilas y funcionales con un tranquilo diseño nórdico ubicadas en el interior de los contenedores marítimos.

Original state

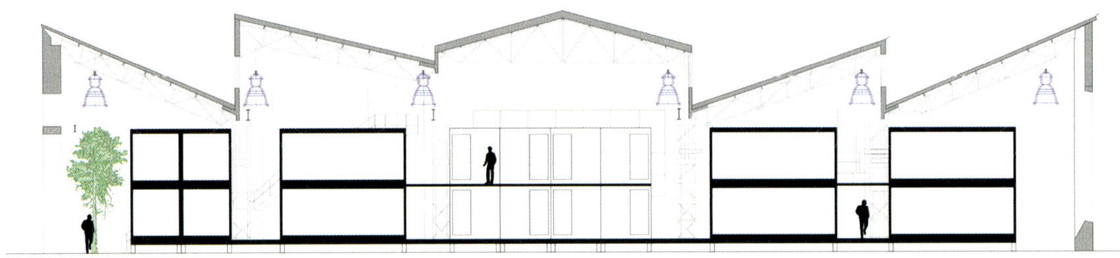

Section

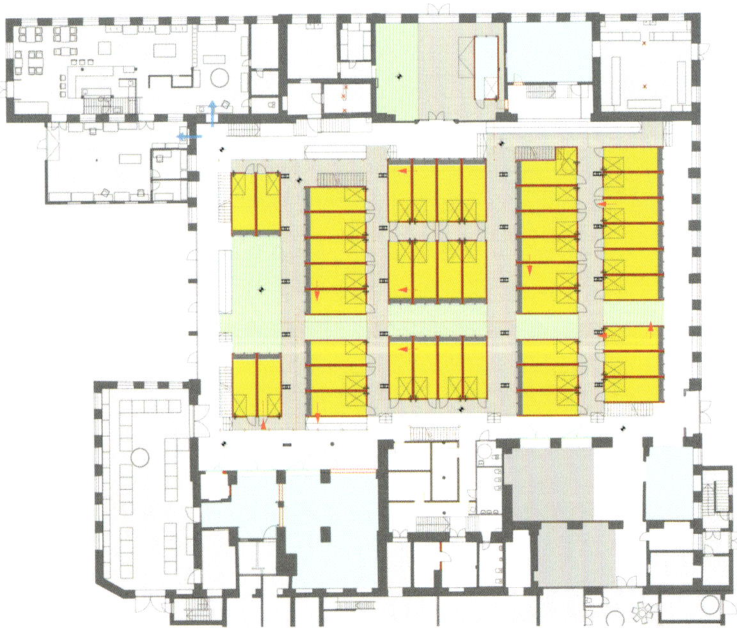

Ground floor plan

First floor plan

Kes mõtleb kastist välja, suudab magada kastis sees!
Those who think outside the box can sleep inside the box!

HOUSE LEMONADE
CONTAINER NEGRONI
GIN & TONIC
GIN SOUR
SKINNY BITCH

CPWU 214
22G
MAX. GR.
TARE
NET
CU. CAP.

CPWU 215043
22G1
MAX GR.
TARE
NET
CU. CAP.

IT SEEMS.
13 000 KG OF PASTA,
MEANS THAT ALL OF
COULD ENJOY A BOWL
BONARA TOGETHER.

DIRECTORY

ARCHIMONTAGE DESIGN FIELDS SOPHISTICATED
www.archimontage.net

MUANGTHONGTHANI CARCARE

LOCATION: Nonthaburi, Thailand
ARCHITECT IN CHARGE: Cherngchai Riawruangsangkul, Thanakit Wiriyasathit
AREA: 330 m^2
PROJECT YEAR: 2019
PHOTOS: © Chaovarith Poonphol Photography

BARAN STUDIO
www.baranstudio.com

MACARTHUR ANNEX

LOCATION: Oakland, California, United States
YEAR COMPLETED: 2017
PROJECT TYPE: Commercial Office & Retail
PROGRAM: 200 sf Shipping Container Units
SQUARE FOOTAGE: 4,581 sf
PHOTOS: © Bénédicte Lassalle

BJB ARCHITECTS
www.bjbarchitects.com.au

BAYS 6-8 HERITAGE OFFICES

LOCATION: Sydney, Australia
ARCHITECT: BJB Architects
LEAD ARCHITECT: Barry Babikian
BUILDER: Infigo
STRUCTURAL ENGINEER: ACOR Consulting
HERITAGE ARCHITECT: Paul Davies
PROJECT COMMISSIONER: Work Inc
ARTIST: Gina Kiel
PHOTOS: ©Mike Chorley Photography

CAZA
www.cazarch.com

ACCESSORY DWELLING UNIT (ADU)

LOCATION: Several locations throughout the USA
COMPLETION YEAR: 2022
GROSS BUILT AREA:
Studio: 400 sf
One Bedroom: 500 sf
PROJECT TEAM: Carlos Arnaiz, Xiao Tan, Queenie Xu, Yihang Yan
CLIENT: Spacial
PHOTOS: © Spacial Homes

DINAMO STUDIO
www.dinamostudio.com

OFICINAS F5.6 / FULFIERROS

LOCATION: San José, Costa Rica
COMPLETION YEAR: 2020
ARCHITECTURAL DESIGN:
Arq. Erick Ledezma Fernández
STRUCTURAL DESIGN:
Ing. Pablo Bolaños Alvarez
ELECTRICAL DESIGN:
Ing. José Adémar Gómez Hidalgo
PLAN DRAWING AND ASSISTANCE:
Arq. Carlos Quesada Vargas
CONSTRUCTION:
Cristián Rojas González.
PHOTOS: © Roberto D'Ambrosio / Fotografía

ECOTECH DESIGN
www. ecotechdesign.com

GENESEO INN

LOCATION: Paso Robles, CA, United States
COMPLETION: 6/2020
PROJECT OWNERS: CASS WINERY: Steve Cass, Ted Plemons
ARCHITECT: Walter Scott Perry
INTERIORS THEMES: Eliana De Leon
CIVIL ENGINEERING: Tim Roberts
CONTAINER ENGINEERING, FABRICATION: CRATE MODULAR
SITE WORK, CONSTRUCTION: TED PLEMONS CONSTRUCTION
PHOTOS AND VIDEO: © HANA, Paul Vu Photographer
RENDERS: James Choe

PALEN STUDIO

LOCATION: Joshua Tree, California, United States
PROJECT OWNER: Tim Palen
ARCHITECT: Walter Scott Perry
INTERIORS: Walter Scott Perry
STRUCTURAL ENGINEERING: Leo Parker, Parker/Resnick Structural Engineers
CONTAINER FABRICATION: 44 WEST CONSTRUCTION
SITE CONSTRUCTION/INSTALLATION: 44 WEST CONSTRUCTION, Eric Engheben
PHOTOS: © JACK PARSONS PHOTOGRAPHY: Jack Parsons
RENDERS: Shawn Keltner

GIANT CONTAINERS
www.giantcontainers.com

STACKT MARKET

LOCATION: Toronto, Canada
COMPLETION YEAR: 2019
Gross Built Area: 100,000 sf
LEAD DESIGNER:
www.lgaarchitecture.com
DESIGN TEAM:
Giant Containers / LGA
CLIENT: Stackt Properties LP
ENGINEERING: Blackwell
CONTRACTOR: Ellis Don
CUSTOM BUILT: Giant Containers
PHOTOS: © Industryous Photography

LOUIS VUITTON MENS TEMPORARY RESIDENCY

LOCATION: Miami, Florida, U.S.A.
COMPLETION YEAR: 2020
GROSS BUILT AREA: 33,000 sf
LEAD DESIGNER: Carla Wells
DESIGN TEAM: Louis Vuitton
CLIENT: Louis Vuitton
ENGINEERING: Bromley Crook
CONTRACTOR: Louis Vuitton / Giant Containers / McKenzie Construction / Eventstar
CUSTOM BUILT: Giant Containers
PHOTOS: © Giant Containers

HADVD ARQUITECTOS
www.had-vd.com

CO°RDENADA CENTRO DE DISEÑO

LOCATION: Ciudad Juárez, Chihuahua, México
YEAR: 2017
BUILT AREA: 420 m^2
DESIGN TEAM: Arq. Hugo A Amparan de León / Arq. Carlos E Villegas Duarte, Arq. Guillermo Morales, LDI Mariana Aguirre, Arq. Víctor Guzmán, Arq. Josimar Bocanegra
FURNITURE: Herman Miller
ARCHITECTURAL PRODUCT: Hunter Douglas
CARPETS AND VINYL FLOORS: Interface
TAPESTRIES: Vescom
PLAFON: Troldtek
PERIMETER WALLS: Novidesa
PHOTOS: © Oscar Hernández

HIGHPOINT TREEHOUSES
www.highpointtreehouses.com

AIR CASTLE

LOCATION: Ladonia, Texas, United States
COMPLETION YEAR: 2019 - 2021
GROSS BUILT AREA: Interior: 750 sf
exterior living space: 900 sf
LEAD DESIGNER: Steve Taylor
DESIGN TEAM: Steve Taylor and Tom Taylor
CLIENT: Steve Taylor
ENGINEERING: Steve Taylor and Gail Rodriquez
CONTRACTOR: Steve Taylor, Jon Ross Wood welding, Billy Underwood Plumbing, L&L Electric, Bonham Glass & Window, Eduardo Hidalgo, Victor Hernández, and Jose Luis Hernández
PHOTOS: © Joe Shipman - Luminous Productions
RENDERINGS: Element One Studio

KG MIMARLIK
www.kgmimarlik.com.tr

KUMPORT

LOCATION: Istanbul, Turkey
LEAD DESIGNER: Kurtul Erkmen
DESIGN TEAM: Büşra Yeltekin, Tilbe Hazal Ağaoğlu, Emre Yiğit, Mesut Özlem, Serhan Günal, Melis Kanadıkırık Savaş
CLIENT: Kumport Liman Hizmetleri ve Lojistik San. ve Tic. A.Ş.
DESIGN, INTERIOR PROJECTS, CONSTRUCTION AND APPLICATION PROJECTS: KG Mimarlık
CONTRACTOR: Yamans Inşaat
GLASS FACADE MATERIAL: Şişecam
STATIC AND STEEL PROJECTS: Büro Statik Mühendislik
MECHANIC AND ELECTRIC PROJECTS: Enve Enerji Mühendislik
PROJECT START: January 2016
PROJECT COMPLETION: August 2016
CONSTRUCTION START: September 2016
CONSTRUCTION COMPLETION: 2018
PLOT AREA: 126.166 m^2
TOTAL BUILT AREA: 7.602 m^2

MEIXNER SCHLÜTER WENDT
www.meixner-schlueter-wendt.de

THE DOCKS

LOCATION: Frankfurt am Main, Germany
PLANNING AND CONSTRUCTION TIME: 2018-2021
GROSS FLOOR AREA: 37,800 m^2
CLIENT: Groß & Partner Grundstücksentwicklungsgesellschaft mbH
PROJECT TEAM: Stepahn Rosa (project architect), Ramon Di Nora, Christine Dörr; Ulrich Domnik, Cordula Fischer, Emanuel Gießen, Chang-Yeh Ho, Angelika Köstler, Felicitas Krätzner, Friederike Sartor, Funda Urungu
STRUCTURAL ENGINEERING: Schüßler Plan
MEP ENGINEERING: Merker AG; Elekrotechnisches Planungsbüro Laber
PHOTOS: Lars Gruber, Christoph Kraneburg, MEIXNER SCHLÜTER WENDT

PAUL MICHAEL DAVIS ARCHITECTS
www.paulmichaeldavis.com

THE WYSS FAMILY CONTAINER HOUSE

LOCATION: Mercer Island, Washington, United States
CLIENTS: Balthasar + Stephanie Wyss
COMPLETION: 2019
AREA: 3200 sf
PRINCIPAL ARCHITECT: Paul Michael Davis
PROJECT DESIGNER: Tiffany Chow
LANDSCAPE: Scott Hallquist, Performance Landscape Company
SHIPPING CONTAINERS: ITS ConGlobal
STRUCTURAL & CIVIL: Mark Leingang, TransOlympic Engineering Inc.
CONTRACTOR: Karlstrom Associates
PROJECT MANAGER: Dick McDonald
SITE SUPERVISOR: Roger Reynolds
PHOTOS: © Mark Woods Photography

RINTALA EGGERTSSON ARCHITECTS
www.ri-eg.com

FLYT. BATHING INSTALLATIONS FOR FLEISCHER PARK

LOCATION: Moss, Norway
CLIENT: Moss municipality
CONSTRUCTION PERIOD:
April to december 2020
CONSTRUCTION BUDGET: NOK 4M
ART COMMITTEE/COMPETITION JURY: Hanne Tollerud, Trygve Nordby, Eva Talberg, Torunn Årset, Silje Hobbel, Berit Kolden and Thale Fastevold
CURATOR: Thale Fastevold
PROJECT MANAGEMENT: Moss municipality: Berit Kolden
DESIGN: Rintala Eggertsson ARCHITECTS: Dagur Eggertsson, Vibeke Jenssen, Mads Øiern, Hanna Hallböök, Johannes Ørn Dagsson, Michele Sicher, Nick Coates, Selma Gulden
ENGINEERING: Multiconsult; Bernt Bakken and Benjamin Henriksen Bjerkeng
LIGHTING DESIGN: SML lighting; Ida Hågensen and Ole Martin Nistad
CONSTRUCTION MANAGMENT: Rintala Eggertsson; Dagur Eggertsson
CONSTRUCTION MAIN STRUCTURE: Sørlaminering: Henrik Aas Hansen. Aanesland: Gunnar Aanesland. Byggmester Tønnes: Tønnes Sindland
CARPENTRY: Dagur Eggertsson, Nick Coates, Selma Gulden, Vibeke Jenssen, Mads Øiern, Solveig Ylva Dagsdottir, Anja Petkovic Karlsen, Torgeir Nordbø, Petri Jäntti, Ditte Horsbøl, Facundo Arboit Diez, Timothy Tan, Rasmus Fjeldheim Dale, Damian Petkovic Karlsen, Lasse Borgos, Dina Watten, Anna Rosa Strassegger and Isak Grimstad
Electricity: Storm Elektro: Morten Bjørkmann, Erik Chi Khan Nguyen and Kristoffer Helgesen
ECONOMIC SUPPORT: The Savingsbank Foundation DNB
SPONSORS: Norsk Stål, Storm Elektro, DuoZink
PHOTOS: © Dag Jenssen, Nicholas Ryan Coates

DRAGONFLY TREEHOTEL

LOCATION: Harads, Sweden
CLIENT: Treehotel
ARCHITECTS: Rintala Eggertsson Architects: Sami Rintala, Dagur Eggertsson, Vibeke Jenssen and Kaori Watanabe
ENGINEER/CONTRACTOR: Vittjärvshus
YEAR: 2013
PHOTOS: © Ryan Koopmans, Peter Lundström

SAFE & GREEN HOLDINGS CORP
www.safeandgreenholdings.com

THE BEACH BOX

LOCATION: Napeague, New York, United States
COMPLETION YEAR: 2012
GROSS BUILT AREA: 2,000 sf
LEAD DESIGNER: Andrew Anderson
DESIGN TEAM: Lawrence Group, Architecture
Client: N/A
ENGINEERING: SG Blocks (Now Safe & Green Holdings Corp)
CONTRACTOR: SG Blocks (Now Safe & Green Holdings Corop)
PHOTOS: © Lena Yaremenko, Marshall Watson

SVA ARCHITECTS. INC.
www.sva-architects.com

POTTER'S LANE PROJECT

LOCATION: Midway City, California,
United States.
COMPLETION YEAR: 2016
GROSS BUILT AREA: 10,187 sf
LEAD DESIGNER: Paul Zaleski
DESIGN TEAM: Robert Simons, Paul Zaleski, Wahid Yonus
CLIENT: American Family Housing
ENGINEERING:
Shipping Container Provider: GrowthPoint Structures
Civil Engineering: J's Engineering
Dry Utilities: tk1sc
Landscape Design: James Dockstader
Cost Estimating: Sierra West Group
CONTRACTOR: Del Amo Construction
AWARDS/DESIGN RECOGNITIONS:
-AIAOC Merit Award: Planned Residential Development
-Builder's Choice & Custom Home Design Awards: Merit Award for Affordable Housing
-PCBC Gold Nugget Award: Best Affordable Housing Community, Judge's Special Award of Excellence
-PCBC Merit Award: Best on the Boards Multifamily Community
-Professional Builder Design Bronze Award: On the Boards Residential or Mixed-Use Project
PHOTOS: © Robert A. Hansen

THOMAS ROSZAK ARCHITECTURE
www.roszak.com

RECESS AND CITY HALL EVENTS

LOCATION: Chicago, Illinois, United States
YEAR: 2020
ARCHITECT OF RECORD:
Thomas Roszak
PROJECT ARCHITECT:
Paul Baulier
STRUCTURAL ENGINEER: Rockey Structures
INTERIOR DESIGNER: Siren Betty
CIVIL ENGINEER: SpaceCo
GENERAL CONTRACTOR:
Aberdeen Contractors
OWNER: Marc Bushala/MAB
PHOTOS: © Sean Henderson

TRAVIS PRICE ARCHITECTS
www.travispricearchitects.com

AARON POMERANTZ BACK YD

LOCATION: Washington DC, USA
COMPLETION YEAR: 2016
GROSS BUILT AREA: 320 sf
LEAD DESIGNER: Travis Price FAIA, Kelly Davies Grace AIA
DESIGN TEAM: Travis Price FAIA, Kelly Davies Grace AIA
CLIENT: Aaron Pomerantz
ENGINEERING: TPA
CONTRACTOR: KGPBuild Inc.
LIGHTING: TPA
PHOTOS: © Ken Wyner

ARUN ARUMUGASWAMY & ARCHANA INKU SHAH RESIDENCE

LOCATION: Silver Spring, Maryland, United States
COMPLETION YEAR: 2020
GROSS BUILT AREA: 3,500 sf
LEAD DESIGNER: Travis Price FAIA, Kelly Davies Grace AIA
DESIGN TEAM: Travis Price FAIA, Kelly Davies Grace AIA
CLIENT: Arun Arumugaswamy
& Archana Inku Shah Residence
ENGINEERING: Kashal
CONTRACTOR: KGPBuild Inc.
LIGHTING: TPA
PHOTOS: © Dan Westergren

BROOKLAND SEAUA APTS

LOCATION: Washington DC, United States
COMPLETION YEAR: 2014
GROSS BUILT AREA: 8500 sfʃ
LEAD DESIGNER: Travis Price, FAIA
DESIGN TEAM: Kelly Davies Grace, AIA
CLIENT: Brookland Equity Group
ENGINEERING: Runkle Consulting Inc
CONTRACTOR: KGP Build
LIGHTING: TPA
PHOTO: © Travis Price Architects, Inc

UDDU DESIGN
www.uddu.ee

LOCATION: Tallinn, Estonia
COMPLETION YEAR: 2020
GROSS BUILT AREA: 2 250 m^2
LEAD DESIGNER: Taavi Aunre / UDDU Design
DESIGN TEAM: Velvet OÜ
CLIENT: Hektor Design Hotels OÜ / Sten Tikk
ENGINEERING: Tero OÜ
CONTRACTOR: Tero OÜ / Ragnar Kruusla
PHOTOS: © Kristjan Mõru, Tiina-Liina Uudam, Terje Ugandi

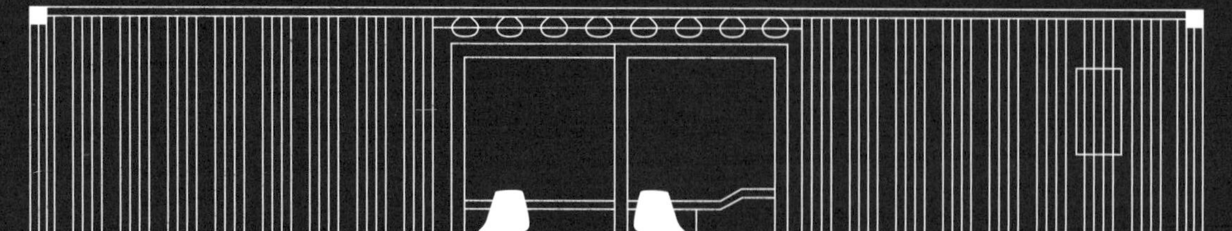